The Law Officers' Departme

Departmen

Presented to Parliament by the Attorney General
and the Chief Secretary to the Treasury
by Command of Her Majesty

May 2006

Cm 6821 £14.75

Contents

Foreword

This report demonstrates the further good progress which the Law Officers' Departments have made during 2005-06 towards delivering my aim of a world-class public service. All the Departments have worked hard to make their individual contributions and I congratulate them on their achievements.

I particularly welcome the report on the first year of the Revenue and Customs Prosecutions Office (RCPO) which was set up on 18 April 2005. RCPO carries forward prosecutions on behalf of HM Revenue and Customs.

Detail of the strategy, which supports my aim, is given later in this report. For the Crown Prosecution Service (CPS), RCPO, Serious Fraud Office (SFO), HM Crown Prosecution Service Inspectorate (HMCPSI) and my own Office, it is part of the wider Vision which the Home Secretary, Lord Chancellor and I have for a fairer, more effective Criminal Justice System (CJS). But the developmental priorities of the strategy are equally important to the Treasury Solicitor's Department (TSol), which provides litigation policy and advisory services to other government departments. The report covers the many activities which each Department has contributed during the last year. I mention a few which demonstrate the progress by which we measure delivery of the strategy.

The prosecution process has been particularly strengthened by the implementation of the Charging programme. This was an ambitious programme which has CPS prosecutors taking charging decisions in all but minor cases. Working with the police, all 42 Areas have been approved to the statutory scheme, a year ahead of schedule. It has helped to contribute to the early achievement of the 2007-08 offences brought to justice target.

In its first year, RCPO has set its standards for presenting high quality prosecutions through its Prosecution Manual; has agreed a Memorandum of Understanding with HM Revenue and Customs, the newly amalgamated investigating department for RCPO cases; and, through a single operating model, has introduced from January 2006 a common prosecution process for cases derived from the former Inland Revenue, HM Customs and Revenue Asset Forfeiture Unit and Customs and Excise Prosecutions Office.

To champion victims, in October 2005, the Code of Practice for Victims of Crime was launched, to come into effect in April 2006. The Code gives the right of appeal should victims feel that agencies have not met their obligations under the Code. Also in October, I introduced the ten-point Prosecutors' Pledge. This identifies the service that victims can expect prosecutors to provide at all stages of the criminal justice process and it will ultimately apply to all prosecutors. The key to **witness care** lies with the 'No Witness No Justice' project. Central to this project are the 165 Witness Care Units which are now available across England and Wales. For cases handled by the Units, the witness attendance rate at trials has increased by 5.5 percentage points and discontinued trials due to witness failure to attend has decreased by 19.9%.

In May 2005, **engaging with communities** was supported by the CPS Community Engagement Strategy, setting out the broad outcomes the CPS wishes to achieve. This will build on the work of specialist prosecutors in anti-social behaviour, operating in 14 CPS Areas. But we have still more work to do, as the outturn against the CJS public confidence target shows.

We have been working trilaterally with CJS colleagues for some years now and **building strong partnerships** has proved its value. In latest developments, the CPS has worked within the cross-CJS Effective Trial Management Programme to introduce the Criminal Case Management Framework. During the year, the proportion of ineffective trials has reduced by 11.3 percentage points in the Crown Court and 9.9 percentage points in the magistrates' courts.

SFO is rightly proud of its reputation in the international field for providing effective and professional mutual legal assistance to overseas authorities within its field. 2005-06 is expected to see the highest level of requests for assistance in four years, the implementation of European directives under the Crime (International Co-operation) Act 2003 accounting for over half.

Becoming an **employer of choice** means offering a challenging and developmental option to other legal work. Since the start of the CPS Law Scholarship Scheme in 2003, 51 scholars have qualified and a recent national campaign for external applicants for the Legal Trainee Scheme attracted over 2,200 applications for 25 places. The Scheme was deservedly recognised in the Personnel Today Award for Excellence in Training. TSol's high reputation continues and its customer care is evidenced by the 97% satisfaction rate achieved for its services in customer surveys.

Together with my Office, the Departments have explored the potential savings from **joining up the Law Officers' Departments** accounting functions, human resources and IT. RCPO now uses the TSol accounting function and my office and SFO have renegotiated a joint IT contract. Shared HR services are also under review.

All the Departments are on course to achieve the 2007-08 **efficiency targets** set in the Spending Review 2004. At 13%, TSol continues to meet its target rate of corporate staff overhead costs, to the benefit of its clients. In 2005-06, HMCPSI completed a new approach to inspection with the first round of its overall performance assessments. As well as identifying instances where CPS Areas might work more effectively, the assessment can also identify where there are likely to be the biggest returns in value for money.

I very much welcome all the achievements of the past year. But I also look to the future and the need for my strategy to be delivered not only effectively but even more efficiently. We shall continue to make efficiency a major factor in providing our world-class service.

Attorney General

Introduction

The Work of the Law Officers' Departments

The Law Officers are the Attorney General and the Solicitor General. They:

- Are principal legal advisers to the Crown and to Ministers;
- Discharge their statutory responsibility for superintendence[1] of the Directors of Public Prosecutions in England and Wales, and Northern Ireland, the Director of the Serious Fraud Office and the Director of the Revenue and Customs Prosecutions Office;
- Have a general oversight of all prosecutions in England and Wales;
- Are Ministers within the CJS together with the Ministers of the Home Office and Department for Constitutional Affairs (DCA).

The Law Officers also have responsibility for bringing certain types of legal proceedings in their own name in the public interest and for granting consent to prosecutions for offences. The Attorney General appoints Advocates to the Court, to assist the courts in civil and criminal proceedings and Special Advocates in proceedings brought before Special Immigration Appeal Commission and in certain other proceedings.

In addition the Attorney General holds the separate post of Attorney General for Northern Ireland. In that role, he superintends the Director of Public Prosecutions for Northern Ireland and appoints and is responsible for the Crown Solicitor.

The Law Officers' Departments comprise the Attorney General's Office (AGO)[2], the CPS and HMCPSI, the RCPO – formerly Customs and Excise Prosecutions Office (CEPO), the SFO and TSol.

The Attorney General's Office is a separate Department, for which the Treasury Solicitor acts as Accounting Officer. Details of its administration are therefore included with those of TSol. AGO provides high-grade legal and strategic policy advice and support to the Law Officers. It ensures appropriate co-ordination across the Law Officers' Departments and contributes towards developing with the CPS, RCPO and SFO the cross-cutting policies of the CJS.

The Crown Prosecution Service, which is headed by the Director of Public Prosecutions, was established by the Prosecution of Offences Act 1985. It is responsible for deciding independently whether criminal proceedings begun by the police in England and Wales should be continued; for deciding the charge in all but minor cases; and for prosecuting those cases it decides to continue.

---

1 Superintendence involves consideration of issues relating to prosecution policy and practice as well as to cases that engage the Law Officers' public interest role.

2 Formerly the Legal Secretariat to the Law Officers.

HM Crown Prosecution Service Inspectorate reports to the Attorney General on the performance of the CPS and the RCPO. Like AGO, details of its administration are included with those of the Treasury Solicitor's Department.

The Revenue and Customs Prosecutions Office, formerly the Customs and Excise Prosecutions Office, was created on 18 April 2005 through the merger of CEPO with the prosecuting arm of the Inland Revenue. CEPO had become accountable to the Attorney General in April 2002, following the recommendation of His Honour John Gower and Sir Anthony Hammond that criminal prosecution work should be independent of the intelligence and investigation work carried out by HM Customs and Excise. A Memorandum of Understanding is being put in place between the Paymaster General on behalf of HM Treasury, the Attorney General, the Commissioners for HM Revenue and Customs and the Director of RCPO concerning the relationship between HM Revenue and Customs and RCPO as to the conduct of criminal investigations and prosecutions by the two departments.

The Serious Fraud Office was established by the Criminal Justice Act 1987. It investigates and prosecutes the most serious or complex cases of fraud in England, Wales and Northern Ireland, thereby contributing to the deterrence of such fraud.

The Treasury Solicitor's Department provides legal services to most Government departments. The Treasury Solicitor is also Head of the Government Legal Service, the organisational name for the legal teams in most central Government bodies.

ATTORNEY GENERAL'S OFFICE and the LAW OFFICERS' DEPARTMENTS: STRUCTURE

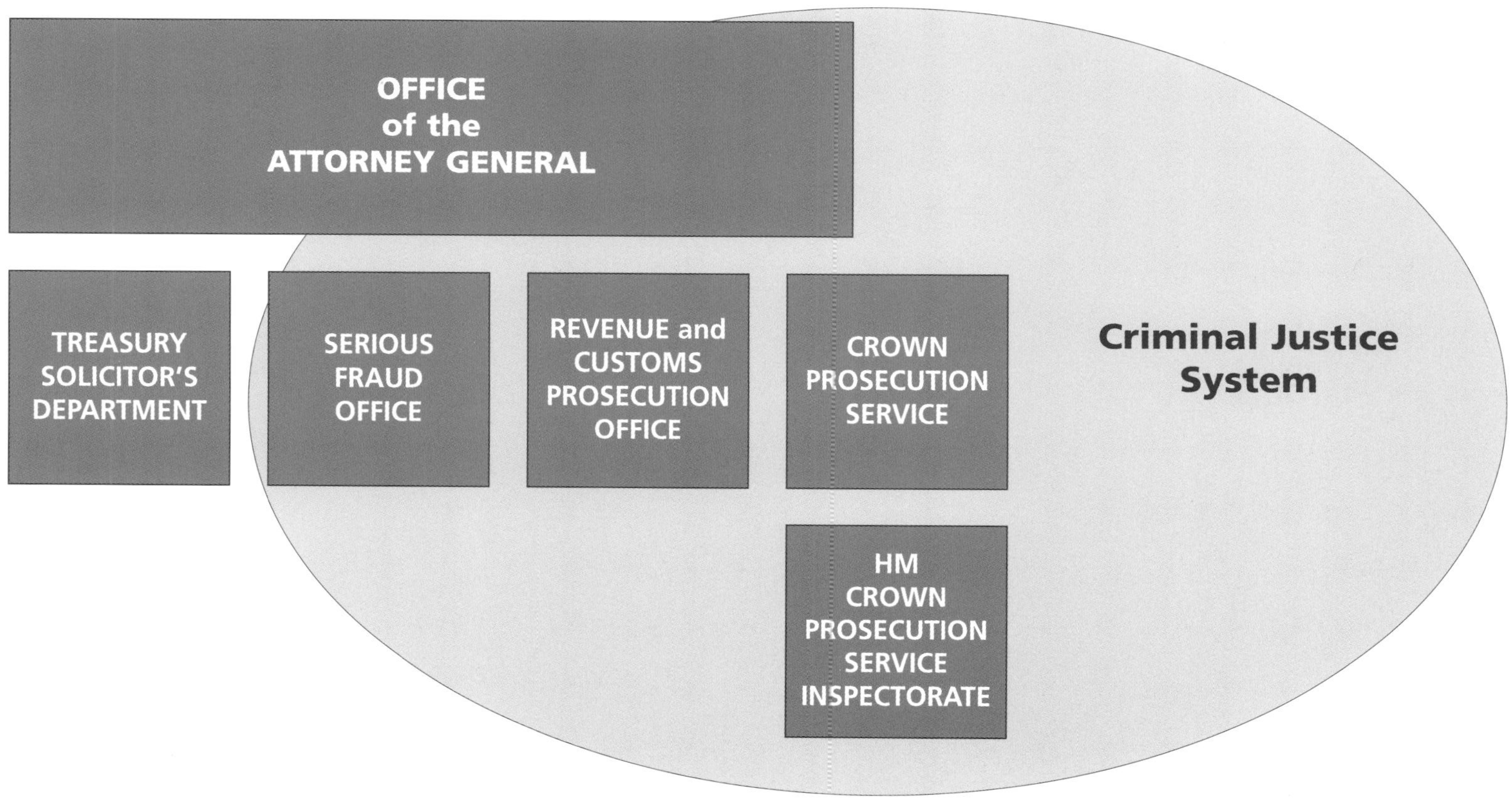

Delivering the Attorney General's Aim – Forward Strategy

Each of the Law Officers' Departments has differing roles, responsibilities and approaches to delivery of their services, tailored to its departmental caseload. But the common vision is to provide world-class public services that meet the needs of victims and communities so that:

- People feel more secure from crime and anti-social behaviour; fewer people's lives are ruined by drugs; and communities are safer places to live and work;
- More offenders are brought to justice and proceeds of crime recovered through a modern and efficient justice process;
- The UK is a more prosperous country because investments are secure and tax revenues protected;
- The public has confidence and trust in the CJS and the work of the Law Officers' Departments;
- Through the performance of the Law Officers' role as the government's chief legal advisers and through the legal services that the Treasury Solicitor provides across government, the best legal support is given to departments in their delivery of quality public services and in their management of their business and people.

The Law Officers with the CPS, RCPO, SFO and HMCPSI are part of the CJS and have joint responsibility with the Home Office and DCA to achieve the delivery of criminal justice targets in the 2004 CJS Public Service Agreement (PSA) which are to:

- Improve the delivery of justice by increasing the number of crimes for which an offender is brought to justice to 1.25 million by 2007-08;
- Reassure the public, reducing the fear of crime and anti-social behaviour, and building confidence in the CJS without compromising fairness.

To deliver the Attorney General's aim, the Ministerial Vision for the wider CJS, and the CJS targets, the prosecuting departments will focus on three service priorities, with plans tailored to the distinct roles of each Law Officers' Department. To increase the capacity to deliver those service priorities, their focus will be on three developmental priorities. The developmental priorities apply equally to TSol in its legal support to other government departments.

Service priorities:

- Strengthening the prosecution process;
- Putting victims and witnesses at the heart of the process;
- Engaging with the communities we serve.

Developmental priorities:

- Building strong partnerships to drive change and delivery across the CJS and shape the CJS of the future;
- Becoming an employer of choice;
- Joining up the Law Officers' Departments better to share common interests and practice.

Strengthening the prosecution process by prosecutors playing an active role from the start to finish of a case, working with the police and other investigators to build the strongest case:

- CPS taking responsibility for Charging with a view to encouraging more guilty pleas; fewer cases being discontinued; and more cases resulting in conviction;
- Conducting pre-trial interviews with witnesses to relate likely evidence to appropriate charges in order to bring more offenders to justice; encourage early guilty pleas; ensure fewer ineffective trials from witness non-attendance; increase witness and victim satisfaction;
- Recovering proceeds of crime through making confiscation the norm where the convicted criminal benefited from the crime; increasing victim satisfaction and public confidence;
- Establishing the RCPO to focus more closely on successful prosecutions and appeals; improving the perceptions of the judiciary and legal community;
- Creating a robust prosecution capacity to complement the establishment of the Serious and Organised Crime Agency (SOCA); to strengthen the response to organised crime; bring faster and more successful extraditions; make more cases subject to asset recovery provisions;
- Active case management with prosecutors constantly reviewing prosecution cases and plugging evidential gaps by working closely with the police and other investigators to build more robust prosecutions; comply with disclosure and other statutory provisions; improve the time within which offenders are brought to justice;
- Electronic presentation of evidence, an essential tool in the prosecution of cases where numbers of witnesses and documents are significant.

Putting victims and witnesses at the heart of the process transforming the approach to victims and witnesses across the CJS. This means giving victims and witnesses more information about decisions and progress; supporting vulnerable victims through the ordeal of going to court; and tackling witness intimidation:

- Improving prosecutors involvement so that the needs of victims and witnesses are identified early improving their willingness to report crimes; reducing ineffective trials; increasing victim and witness satisfaction; and improving conviction through better quality evidence;
- Effective trial management with prosecutors providing a single point of contact for victims; giving more and better information to witnesses; leading to fewer adjournments;
- Ensuring the victim's voice is heard in court by prosecutors presenting the views of the victim; challenging inaccurate and unfair mitigation so that offenders receive appropriate sentences and the victim and community feel increased reassurance.

Engaging with communities so that prosecutors actively seek the views of the community when shaping prosecution policies:

- Community Justice programmes, with prosecutors working with police, courts, local authorities and social services to tackle anti-social behaviour and low-level criminality highlighted by local communities and local crime and disorder partnerships;
- Taking forward Community Engagement Strategies;

These proposals should ensure a reduction in anti-social behaviour, an increase in public confidence and encourage more people to come forward to report and give evidence against crime.

Building strong partnerships, through prosecution being at the centre of many mutual dependencies within the CJS and looking outward towards the international community:

- Greater contribution to national bodies and Local Criminal Justice Boards;
- A clearer role for all prosecutors including determining the role to be played by the SFO and RCPO within the CJS and integrating them into CJS partnerships;
- Criminal justice reform measures that are informed by experience across the frontline;
- International co-operation, acknowledging that crime does not respect national boundaries;
- A joined-up Inspection regime.

The impact of effective partnerships will be seen in the delivery of the CJS targets.

Employer of choice reflects the commitment to making the Law Officers' Departments places to which some of the brightest and most committed professionals are attracted, to pursue rewarding and interesting careers and be recognised and respected for offering a valued service:

- More Higher Courts Advocates in the Crown Court;
- More Designated Caseworkers presenting a wide range of cases in the magistrates' courts;
- Regular review of equality and diversity polices to achieve a representative workforce and a reputation for fairness in employment as well as comply with legislation;
- Legal trainee and scholarship schemes offering opportunity to those with the talent and desire to qualify as prosecutors;
- Developing leadership and management skills of senior staff;
- Having the ultimate goal that prosecutors will be eligible to apply for judicial Crown Court appointments, improving career progression for lawyers and opening up an untapped reservoir of talent and diverse applicants.

Success will be measured by more effective prosecutions; improved British Crime Survey statistics on public confidence; increasingly positive feedback from judiciary and staff attitude surveys; levels of credible applications for vacancies; and improvements in sick absence rates.

Joining up the Law Officers' Departments to communicate best practice, identify efficiencies and, where appropriate, re-direct resources to improve frontline delivery:

- Identifying efficiencies in co-operation over administrative functions;
- Looking to common IT solutions;
- Sharing training and transferring skills between departments; and looking at the feasibility of a professional accreditation for non-legal staff;
- Reviewing governance structures following the creation of RCPO and changes in HMCPSI, in particular the way risk is managed.

Success will be measured by achieving departmental value for money targets.

1

Crown Prosecution Service
Crown Prosecution Service Tables

CROWN PROSECUTION SERVICE

Introduction

Role

The Crown Prosecution Service (CPS) was set up in 1986 as an independent authority to prosecute criminal cases investigated by the police in England and Wales. In this role, the CPS:

- Advises the police during the early stages of investigations;
- Determines the appropriate charges in all but minor cases;
- Keeps all cases under continuous review and decides which cases should be prosecuted;
- Prepares cases for prosecution in court, prosecutes the case with in-house advocacy or instructs agents and counsel to present cases; and
- Provides information and assistance to victims and prosecution witnesses.

Code for Crown Prosecutors

Before charging a defendant and proceeding with a prosecution, Crown Prosecutors must first review each case against the Code for Crown Prosecutors. The Code sets out the principles the CPS applies in its work, whether:

- There is enough evidence to provide a realistic prospect of conviction against each defendant on each charge and; if so,
- A prosecution is needed under the public interest.

The Director is under a statutory duty to publish the Code for Crown Prosecutors. The fifth edition of the Code was published on 16 November 2004 and reflects the new responsibilities for Crown Prosecutors to determine charges.

Human Rights Act

The CPS is a public authority for the purposes of the Human Rights Act 1998. Crown Prosecutors must apply the principles of the European Convention on Human Rights in accordance with the Act.

Organisation

The CPS is headed by the Director of Public Prosecutions (DPP), Ken Macdonald QC. The Director is superintended by the Attorney General who is accountable to Parliament for the Service. The Chief Executive is Richard Foster, who is responsible for running the business on a day-to-day basis, and for human resources, finance, business information systems, and business development, allowing the Director to concentrate on prosecution, legal issues and criminal justice policy.

CPS Areas

The CPS has 42 Areas across England and Wales. Each Area is headed by a Chief Crown Prosecutor (CCP) who is responsible for the delivery of a high quality prosecution service to the local community. Each CCP is supported by an Area Business Manager (ABM) and their respective roles mirror, at a local level, the responsibilities of the DPP and the Chief Executive. Administrative support to Areas is provided through a network of business centres. A 'virtual' 43rd Area, CPS Direct, also headed by a CCP, provides out-of-hours charging advice to the police.

Specialised prosecution work is undertaken by three casework divisions based in CPS Headquarters, dealing with issues such as serious organised crime, terrorism and other specialised prosecution cases.

Links with Local Criminal Justice Boards

Local Criminal Justice Boards (LCJBs) bring together the Chief Officers of local criminal justice agencies to deliver the Public Service Agreement (PSA) targets in their Area and to drive through criminal justice reforms. Each LCJB has produced delivery plans to bring more offenders to justice, reduce ineffective trials and increase public confidence. Progress on the plans is reported to the National Criminal Justice Board (NCJB). The Attorney General, Solicitor General, DPP and CPS Chief Executive, along with the Home Secretary, Lord Chancellor and others, are members of the NCJB.

Office for Criminal Justice Reform

The CPS also works closely with the Office for Criminal Justice Reform (OCJR), which is the trilateral team drawn from the Home Office, Department for Constitutional Affairs (DCA) and CPS to support criminal justice departments, agencies and LCJBs in working together to deliver PSA targets and to improve the service provided to the public.

Police Reform

The CPS is working closely with the Home Office and DCA on the recently announced Police Reform proposals. It is reviewing its organisation in readiness to respond to police force restructuring and ensure the CPS continues to provide a high quality prosecuting service in partnership with the police.

Management Structure

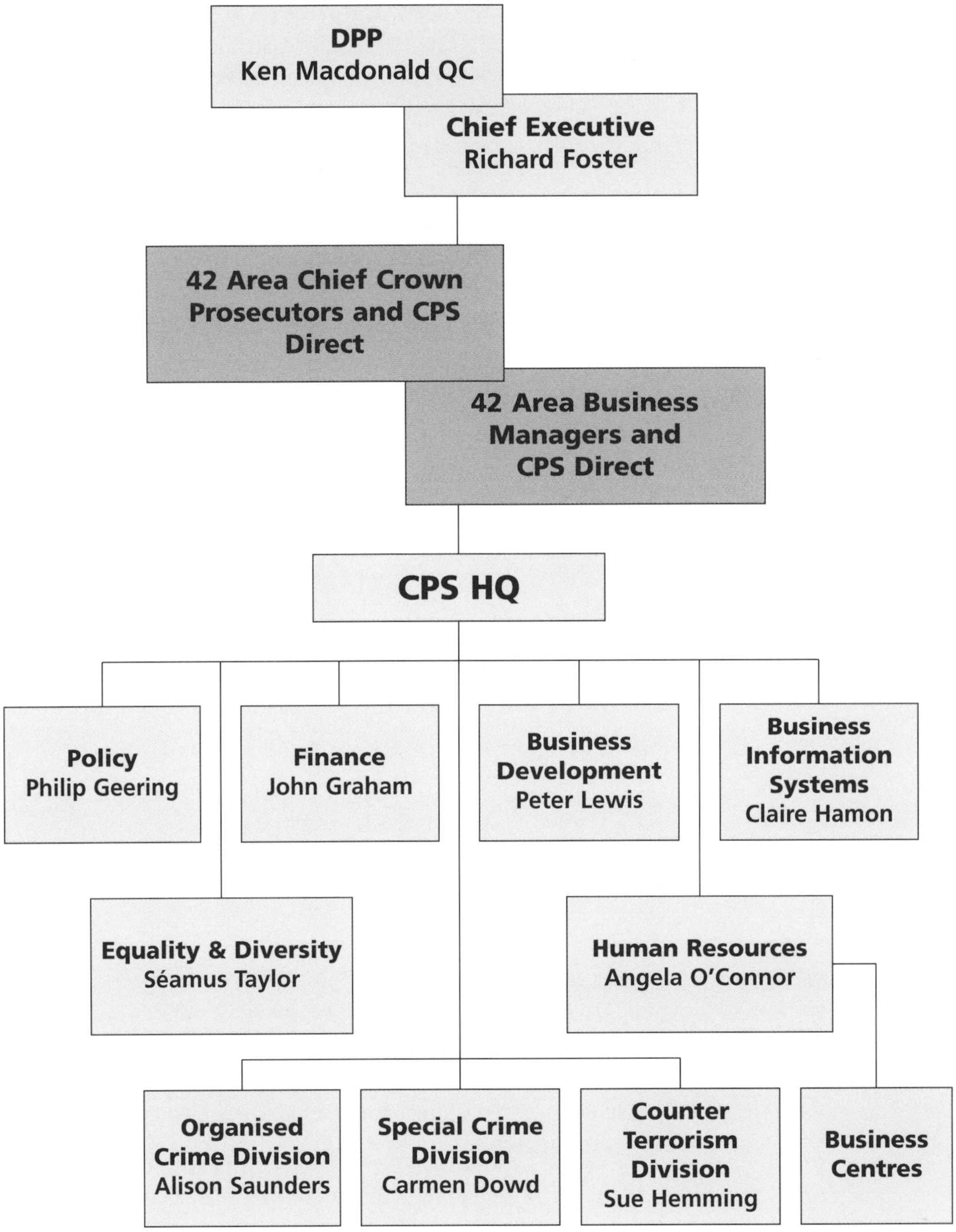

Aim

The CPS works in partnership with the Home Office, DCA, Revenue and Customs Prosecutions Office, Serious Fraud Office, police, courts and other agencies throughout the Criminal Justice System (CJS) to reduce crime, the fear of crime, and its social and economic cost; to dispense justice fairly and efficiently and to promote confidence in the rule of law.

The CPS's aim, which reflects the Government's priorities for the CJS and the Attorney General's for the Law Officers' Departments, is to:

Deliver a high quality prosecution service that brings offenders to justice, helps reduce both crime and the fear of crime and thereby promote public confidence in the rule of law through the consistent fair and independent review of cases and through their fair, thorough and firm presentation at court.

CPS Vision

The CPS aspires to be a world-class, independent prosecuting authority, at the heart of the CJS, providing a valued public service that meets the needs of victims, witnesses and communities, making a real difference to the lives of local people and helping to build a fairer and more decent society. This will be a Service that:

- Strengthens the prosecution process to bring offenders to justice;
- Champions justice and the rights of victims;
- Inspires the confidence of the communities we serve;
- Drives change and delivery in the CJS;
- Is renowned for fairness, excellent career opportunities and the commitment and skills of all its people; and
- Has a strong capability to deliver.

Criminal Justice System Performance

Public Service Agreement Targets

PSA targets were set for the CJS in the Spending Review 2004 (SR 2004) for 2005-08. The targets, reported on at pages 17-18, are the responsibility of the Home Office, DCA and the CPS. Similar PSA targets were also set in the Spending Review 2002 (SR 2002) for 2003-06 and are reported on at pages 21-22. The relationship between the SR 2002 and the SR 2004 targets is shown below.

PSA Targets Progression Map

SR 2002	SR 2004
PSA 1 To improve the delivery of justice by increasing the number of crimes for which an offender is brought to justice, to 1.15 million by 2005-06, with an improvement in all CJS areas, a greater increase in the worst performing areas, and a reduction in the proportion of ineffective trials.	**PSA 1** Improve the delivery of justice by increasing the number of offences for which an offender is brought to justice to 1.25 million for 2007-08.
PSA 2 To improve the level of public confidence in the CJS, including increasing that of ethnic minority communities, and increasing year on year the satisfaction of victims and witnesses, whilst respecting the rights of defendants.	**PSA 2** Reassure the public, reducing the fear of crime and anti-social behaviour, and building confidence in the CJS without compromising fairness.

Efficiency Savings

SR 2004 also requires the CPS to deliver £34 million efficiency savings by March 2008 (pages 19-20). Additionally the value for money PSA target set in SR 2002 is still being taken forward (page 22). The CPS has no workforce reduction target in SR 2004, but has a target of relocating 20 posts by 2010.

SR 2004 Progress on Delivery

PSA Target 1:

Improve the delivery of justice by increasing the number of offences for which an offender is brought to justice to 1.25 million for 2007-08.

'Offences brought to justice' counts the number of offences for which someone is convicted, cautioned, has had taken into consideration by the court, or for which they receive a penalty notice (for some disorder cases), or a formal warning for possession of cannabis. Only notifiable offences are counted.

Performance Measures	Latest Outturn
Increasing the number of offences for which an offender is brought to justice.	**Ahead**

Performance Measures

Increasing the number of offences for which an offender is brought to justice.

The target will be met if there are 1.25 million crimes for which an offender is brought to justice in the year ending March 2008.

The target for the period 2005-06 is to bring 1.15 million offences to justice. This target was modified in SR 2004 superseding the previous target of 1.2 million offences brought to justice in 2005-06. At the same time, a higher target of 1.25 million offences brought to justice was set for 2007-08.

Latest Outturn

Ahead

Latest performance on offenders brought to justice is 1.267 million[3] in the year ending December 2005. This is 26.4% above baseline. Performance must be maintained but provisional data shows that we are already ahead of the 2007-08 target level.

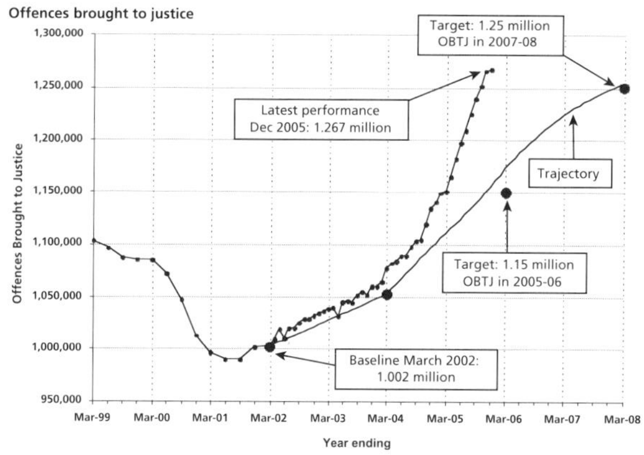

[3] This figure is provisional and subject to change.

PSA Target 2:

Reassure the public, reducing the fear of crime and anti-social behaviour, and building confidence in the CJS without compromising fairness.

Public confidence in the CJS and the satisfaction of victims and witnesses is assessed using the British Crime Survey (BCS) and the Home Office Citizenship Survey (HOCS).

Responsibility for the three assurance elements of the target lies with the Home Office. The three confidence elements, reported on below, are shared between the Home Office, DCA and the CPS.

Performance Measures	Latest Outturn	
Improve the level of public confidence in the CJS. This is determined using questions in the BCS which ask whether the public believes the CJS is effective in bringing people who commit crimes to justice.	**Ahead.**	
	Baseline (BCS 2002-03):	39%
	Target (BCS 2007-08):	An increase
	Annual Outturn (BCS 2004-05):	43%
	Latest Outturn (Year to December 2005):	44%
Reduce the number of people in ethnic minority communities who believe the CJS would treat them worse than people of other races. This is determined using questions in the Home Office Citizenship Survey which ask whether people from a black or minority ethnic background believe the CJS would treat them worse than people of other races.	**On Course.**	
	Baseline (HOCS 2001):	33%
	Target (HOCS 2007):	A reduction
	Latest Outturn (HOCS 2005):	31%
Increasing satisfaction of victims and witnesses. This is measured using BCS questions on victim and witness satisfaction with the CJS.	**On Course.**	
	Baseline (BCS six months to March 2004):	58%
	Target (BCS 2007-08):	An increase
	Annual Outturn (BCS 2004-05):	59%
	Latest Outturn (Year to December 2005):	59%

Delivering Efficiencies

To achieve the SR 2004 efficiency target of £34.1m by March 2008, the CPS plans to deliver efficiencies of £20 million in 2005-06, £27 million in 2006-07 and £34 million in 2007-08. The table below shows these yearly plans, along with the discrete year savings made in 2004-05 and 2005-06 to date.

Workstream	2004-05		2005-06		2006-07	2007-08	
	CPS Plan	*Actual*	CPS Plan	*Actual to date**	CPS Plan	SR2004 Target	Cashable
Charging Programme	10.0	*15.6*	15.0	*18.1*	17.5	20.0	17.5
Productive Time	1.3	*2.4*	3.8	*7.0*	6.1	8.1	4.6
Procurement	0.3	*2.5*	0.5	*3.4*	1.0	2.5	5.3
Corporate Services	–	–	0.8	*0.8*	2.0	3.5	0.8
Total	**11.6**	***20.5***	**20.1**	***29.3***	**26.6**	**34.1**	**28.2**

** To December 2005*

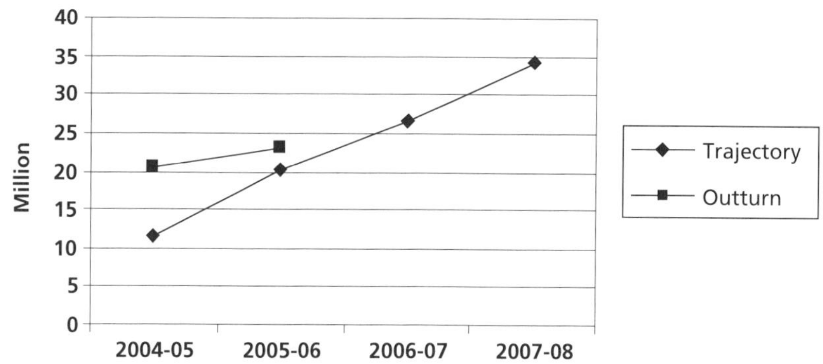

The targets will be delivered through planned initiatives, broadly covering:

- The implementation of the charging programme, designed to improve the effectiveness and the efficiency of the criminal justice process, it is measured by success in terms of the improvement in the guilty plea rate, reductions in discontinuance and reductions in the proportion of cases that do not result in a conviction;
- Improvements in productive time, measured through a survey of users of the COMPASS Management Information System and in the deployment of Higher Courts Advocates (HCAs) and Designated Caseworkers (DCWs);

- Improving procurement practices, which focus on reducing the costs of goods and services by developing structured specification for goods and services for a range of suppliers whilst ensuring the quality of goods and services is maintained; and
- Savings through HQ rationalisation, relocation and corporate services reorganisation, where service levels and process quality have been assessed and benchmarked. The savings are measured through the number of staff redeployed, overhead cost comparison, and transaction processing costs.

The CPS expects the charging programme to account for around 60 per cent of planned savings by 2007-08, with another 20 per cent coming from productive time efficiencies and the remainder through improved efficiency in the provision of corporate services and savings delivered through more effective procurement practices. Cashable savings are being re-invested in charging, COMPASS and the Case Management System, and meeting new workload pressures on frontline staff.

Actions taking place to deliver efficiencies

- All 42 CPS Areas are now operating under the new Statutory Charging arrangements which were introduced by the Criminal Justice Act 2003.
- The structural reorganisation of Service Centres has been completed, including reducing the number of Service Centres to deliver services to Areas as efficiently and effectively as possible.
- The COMPASS programme successfully passed an Office of Government Commerce (OGC) led Gateway Review 5 on benefits realisation. The COMPASS benefits annual report for 2004-05 was published in July 2005.
- HCA pathfinder sites in CPS Hertfordshire and Hampshire & Isle of Wight reached the interim evaluation stage and both sites recorded significant successes. All Areas are implementing local plans to increase the use of HCAs and DCWs as part of a strategy to increase CPS in-house advocacy.
- Procurement initiatives are being implemented and are on course to meet the 2005-06 savings target of £0.5 million as well as the targets for future years.
- Good progress has already been made on the relocation target, which has already been met with 43 posts relocated to date.

Plans for delivering efficiencies over the next 6-12 months

- Following the rollout of the Statutory Charging programme to all 42 Areas, final assurance checks and post implementation reviews will continue.
- The benefits realisation plans and funding for the COMPASS programme for 2006-07 will be agreed with Criminal Justice IT (CJIT) and HM Treasury.
- The Service Centre Review project will complete the programme of redeploying all displaced staff. New Business Centres will have service level agreements in place with Areas and with HQ.
- Continuous review and re-negotiation of supplier contracts will continue to ensure that challenging efficiency delivery targets for procurement are met.
- New targets for HCA and DCW deployment for future years will be set in the light of experience to date.

SR 2002 Progress on Delivery

PSA Target 1:

To improve the delivery of justice by increasing the number of crimes for which an offender is brought to justice, to 1.15 million by 2005-06, with an improvement in all CJS Areas, a greater increase in the worst performing Areas and a reduction in the proportion of ineffective trials.

'Ineffective trials' are trials that do not go ahead on the date expected and have to be rescheduled.

'Unsuccessful outcomes' are finalised cases that do not result in a conviction, such as discontinuances in magistrates' courts cases and judge directed acquittals in the Crown Court.

Performance Measures	Latest Outturn
Increasing the number of offences for which an offender is brought to justice. *The target will be met if there are 1.15 million offences for which an offender is brought to justice in the year ending March 2006, compared with the baseline year ending March 2002.* *This aspect of the target was modified in SR 2004, superseding the previous target of 1.2 million offences brought to justice in 2005-06.*	**Ahead.** Latest performance on offenders brought to justice is 1.267 million[4] in the year ending December 2005. This is 26.4% above baseline. Performance must be maintained but we have already achieved our interim 2005-06 target.
An improvement in all CJS Areas. *The target will be met if, in each of the 42 Criminal Justice Areas, more offences are brought to justice in 2005-06 than in the baseline year 2001-02.*	**On Course.** For the year ending December 2005, 39 areas were performing at a level ahead of their March 2002 baselines.[5]
A greater increase in worst performing Areas. *The target will be met if the average performance improvement achieved by the worse performing Criminal Justice Areas between 2001-02 and 2005-06 is greater than the national average performance improvement for the same period.*	**On Course.** 18 areas have been classified as 'worse performing'. For the year ending December 2005, the aggregated performance of these areas was on track to achieve the target.[6]
A reduction in the proportion of ineffective trials. *The target will be met if the national level of ineffective trials is reduced from 24% to 17% (March 2006) for Crown Courts and from 31% to 23% (March 2006) for magistrates' courts.*	**Ahead.** At January 2006 the proportion of ineffective trials in the Crown Court Centres had reduced from 24% (baseline) to 12.7%, an improvement of 11.3 percentage points. For magistrates' courts the proportion of ineffective trials has reduced from 31% to 21.1% in the quarter ending January 2006, an improvement of 9.9 percentage points. Current performance is the best to date and the figures are already at the March 2006 target level.

[4] This figure is provisional and subject to change.
[5&6] This data is provisional and is subject to minor revision. The figures quoted here were correct at 13 March 2006.

PSA Target 2:

To improve the level of public confidence in the CJS, including increasing that of ethnic minority communities, and increasing year on year the satisfaction of victims and witnesses, whilst respecting the rights of defendants.

Performance Measures	Latest Outturn
Improve the level of public confidence in the CJS.	**Ahead.** Baseline (BCS 2002-03): 39% Target (BCS 2005-06): An increase Annual Outturn (BCS 2004-05): 43% Latest Outturn (Year to December 2005): 44%
– including increasing that of ethnic minority communities.	**Ahead.** Baseline (BCS 2002-03): 49% Target (BCS 2005-06): An increase Annual Outturn (BCS 2004-05): 56% Latest Outturn (Year to December 2005): 57%
– increasing year on year the satisfaction of victims.	**Slippage.** Baseline (BCS six months to March 2004): 59% Target (BCS 2005-06): An increase Annual Outturn (BCS 2004-05): 58% Latest Outturn (Year to December 2005): 59%
– increasing year on year the satisfaction of witnesses.	**On Course.** Baseline (BCS six months to March 2004): 57% Target (BCS 2005-06): An increase Annual Outturn (BCS 2004-05): 58% Latest Outturn (Year to December 2005): 59%
– whilst respecting the rights of defendants.	The rights of defendants are protected by law. We will investigate and take action if there is any evidence that the rights of defendants are not being respected or that public confidence in rights being respected is falling.

PSA Target 3:

To increase value for money from the CJS by 3 per cent a year.

Performance Measures	Latest Outturn
To increase value for money from the CJS by 3% per annum. *The CPS contribution to the target will be met if by year ending March 2006, there is an improvement in efficiency or value for money of at least 3% compared with the year ending March 2003.* Some CPS-led initiatives have efficiency and value for money benefits for the police and the courts as well as the CPS.	The CPS increased value for money and made efficiency savings for re-investment in frontline prosecution services through: • The introduction of charging arrangements; • Improved use of the COMPASS Case Management System; • Increased use of HCAs and DCWs; • Reduction in the use of agents in the magistrates' courts; • Improvements to the management of leases on the estate; and • Improved terms from suppliers as a result of introducing online ordering and procurement.

CPS Performance

People

At the end of December 2005, the CPS employed a total of 8,138 people, 342 more than at the same time the previous year. This includes 2,717 prosecutors and 4,697 caseworkers and administrators. Over 91% of all staff are engaged in, or support, frontline prosecutions. The CPS has 563 prosecutors able to advocate in the Crown Court and on cases in the Higher Courts and 263 DCWs able to present cases in magistrates' courts.

Workload

In 2005, the CPS provided 558,087 pre-charge decisions, completed 1,082,989 cases in magistrates' courts, and a further 91,326 cases in the Crown Court. This compares with 2004-05 workload of 441,194 pre-charge decisions, 1,168,078 completed cases in the magistrates' courts and 94,737 cases in the Crown Court.

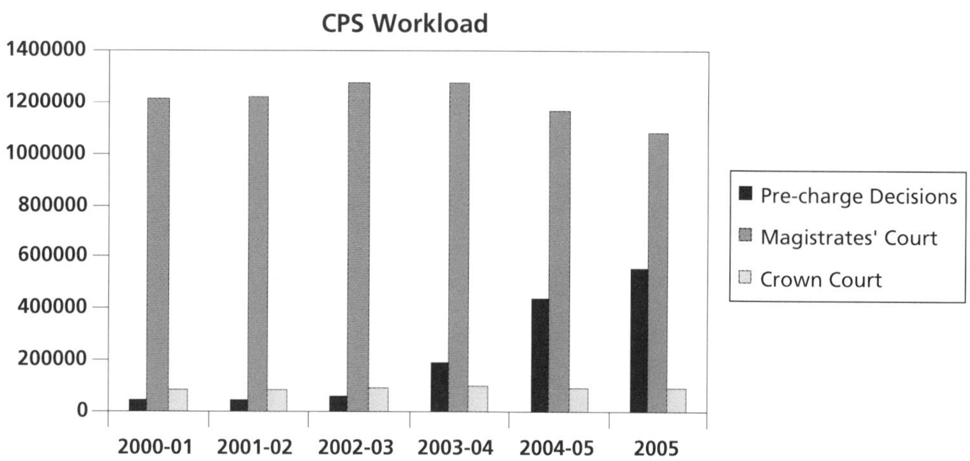

Case Outcomes

There were continued improvements in reducing unsuccessful cases. Magistrates' courts unsuccessful outcomes represented 17.6% of the total compared with 19.2% in the preceding year. Crown Court unsuccessful outcomes represented 23% of the total, compared with a figure of 24.2% in 2004-05.

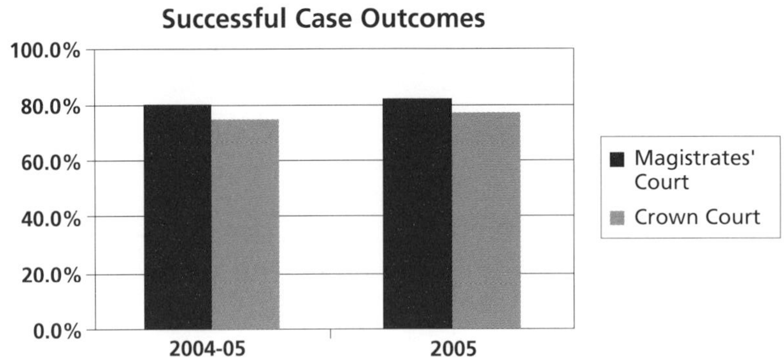

Resources

The CPS budget for 2005-06 to 2007-08 was set in the SR 2004:

£ million	SR 2004 Baseline Provision			
	2004-05 Outturn	2005-06 Forecast Outturn	2006-07 Plans	2007-08 Plans
Administration Costs	57	55	58	58
Programme Costs	508	548	537	574
Total	**565**	**603**	**595**	**632**

Over the three years up to 2007-08, the SR 2004 settlement represents an average increase in real terms of 3 per cent a year. From 2005-06 onwards, HM Treasury has agreed to switch frontline costs, currently classified as administration costs, into programme costs. The baseline provision does not include the anticipated use of end year flexibility.

Because of additional funding from the Invest to Save Budget for No Witness No Justice (NWNJ), CJIT for development of COMPASS Case Management System and to support NWNJ, and funds from the Home Office for Charging and the implementation of the Proceeds of Crime Act and other initiatives, expenditure in 2005-06 is significantly higher than the original baseline provision of £557 million.

The SR 2004 settlement requires the CPS to:

- Deliver more challenging PSA targets;
- Pay for the cost of the rollout of full statutory charging across England and Wales;
- Improve the handling of victims and witnesses, promote their needs, ensure that victims' views are represented and enable both victims and witnesses to give evidence effectively; and
- Deliver significant efficiency savings of £34 million by 2008.

Regulatory Impact Assessments

The CPS is not a regulatory department but does contribute to Home Office impact assessments on criminal justice legislation and DCA impact assessments when appropriate.

Modernising the Law Officers' Departments

Attorney General's Vision

The Attorney General's Vision for the Law Officers' Departments aims to:

- Strengthen the prosecution process;
- Put victims and witnesses at the heart of the process;
- Engage with the communities we serve;
- Build strong partnerships to drive change and delivery across the CJS and shape the CJS of the future;
- Become an employer of choice; and
- Join up the Law Officers' Departments better to share common interests and practice.

Strengthening the Prosecution Process

Charging

The Criminal Justice Act 2003 gave the CPS responsibility for the decision to charge in all but minor cases. The SR 2004 settlement required the delivery of Statutory Charging across all 42 Areas by March 2007.

Working in partnership with the Association of Chief Police Officers (ACPO) and local police forces, Statutory Charging arrangements are now in place in all police custody units across England and Wales, with 276 of them providing face-to-face advice. Statutory Charging was implemented first in the Government's thirteen priority Areas and Cleveland, where the majority of recorded crime takes place in England and Wales. All the priority Areas successfully migrated to the statutory scheme by November 2004. By 3 April 2006, all 42 Areas had been approved onto the statutory scheme – almost twelve months ahead of the SR 2004 target date.

The charging arrangements are already delivering considerable benefits, with prosecutors working closely with the police to build robust cases for prosecution that are helping to bring more offences to justice, increase guilty pleas and reduce the number of cases that are discontinued.

CPS Direct

Area charging arrangements are supported by CPS Direct, an out-of-hours telephone service that allows experienced prosecutors to work from their own homes to provide the police with charging advice through the night and at weekends. By the end of March 2006, the 123 prosecutors working for CPS Direct had dealt with 157,150 out-of-hours calls from police forces and provided 96,108 advices on the charges to be applied.

Advocacy

As part of becoming a world-class prosecuting service the CPS is developing its own high quality advocacy in all courts. During 2005-06, HCAs in the two pathfinder projects in Hertfordshire and Hampshire and Isle of Wight, continued to advocate more cases in the Crown Court, with HCAs covering approximately 50% of non-contested and 22% of contested Crown Court hearings.

In the first three quarters of 2004-05 the value of HCA generated counsel fee savings was £1,189,400 (ex VAT), equating to 2.1% of the total Crown Court Graduated Fee Scheme (GFS) advocacy value. During the same period in 2005-06, the value of HCA generated counsel fee savings was £3,176,489 (ex VAT), equating to 5.9% of the total Crown Court GFS advocacy value. The number of trials conducted by HCAs nationally in the first three quarters of 2005-06 has increased from 20 to 75.

The DPP issued revised General Instructions to DCWs in relation to magistrates' courts advocacy, which came into force on 2 January 2006. DCWs may now conduct contested bail hearings and pre-trial reviews in magistrates' courts. The new powers were used initially in London and Humberside, the early implementation Areas. Following national rollout of a new training programme, DCWs in all Areas are now able to exercise the full range of powers.

Prosecuting Serious, Organised and International Crime

In preparation for the Serious Organised Crime Agency (SOCA), which became fully operational on 1 April 2006, the CPS has restructured its Casework Directorate into three new Divisions to deal with counter-terrorism, organised crime and specialised crimes.

From September 2005, the Organised Crime Division (OCD) assumed responsibility for all new cases referred to the CPS by the National Crime Squad (NCS), as well as taking on some existing NCS cases being dealt with by CPS Areas. A feature of the new arrangements is very early involvement of prosecutors in NCS operations, to ensure that strong cases can be built from the outset of an investigation.

Counter Terrorism Division (CTD) deals with all terrorist related cases throughout England and Wales. Specialist Prosecutors in CTD also deal with cases of incitement to racial hatred, crimes against humanity and Official Secrets Act cases.

The Special Crime Division (SCD) is responsible for prosecuting and assisting the prosecution of a range of the most sensitive, specialised and novel cases. SCD prosecutes cases where for operational and/or resourcing reasons, work needs to be undertaken at Headquarters rather than in the Areas. This may include the extradition of a defendant from overseas, or where a case is made the subject of an appeal to the House of Lords.

Disclosure

Disclosure is the process through which the prosecution reviews and then provides the defence with unused material which might reasonably be considered capable of undermining the case for the prosecution against the accused, or of assisting the case for the accused. The Disclosure Manual was fully revised, extended in scope, and re-published in April 2005 to reflect the prosecution team approach to the disclosure process, moving through investigations, advice and charge, to prosecution. The Manual also contains guidance to deal with the most sensitive and complex disclosure issues arising in serious, organised and cross border crime. The CPS has contributed extensively to the development of a Judicial Protocol on disclosure and is currently participating in an inter-departmental review of third party material.

Casework Quality Assurance

CPS Headquarters routinely assesses the quality of casework being produced in Areas by using a sampling and assessment process called 'Casework Quality Assurance'. Each month sample case files are examined and tested against a range of standard questions at key stages of the prosecution process. The scheme helps managers to identify casework that fails to meet a satisfactory standard and where further staff training or development is required.

The scheme has been adopted across the CPS with about 19,000 files being examined each year. The results of the monitoring indicate that a good level of casework quality is being maintained across the Service, with over 94.4% of cases showing a proper application of the Code, CPS policy and charging standards.

Pre-trial Interviews

The piloting of pre-trial witness interviews began in CPS Cumbria, Greater Manchester, Lancashire and Merseyside in January 2006. Experienced and specially trained prosecutors now have the opportunity to assess the reliability of, or clarify, a witness's evidence prior to charge or trial. The pilots will run until 30 September 2006, when they will be independently evaluated and a decision will be taken on rollout to all Areas.

Championing Victims and Witnesses

Prosecutors' Pledge

On 21 October 2005, the Attorney General introduced a ten-point Prosecutors' Pledge that sets out the level of service that victims can expect to receive from prosecutors. This includes considering the impact of a crime on the victim or their family when making a charging decision, promoting and encouraging two-way communications between a victim and a prosecutor, and after a conviction applying for compensation, restitution or future protection of the victim where appropriate. The Pledge underpins the new Attorney General's Guidelines outlining the important role that prosecutors play in protecting victims' interests at key stages of the criminal justice process, in particular in accepting pleas and at sentencing.

Victims' Code

The Code of Practice for Victims of Crime (The Victims' Code) was launched in October 2005, as part of the Domestic Violence Crime and Victims Act 2004, and came into full effect on 4 April 2006. The Code sets out the services victims can expect to receive from the CJS, including notifying vulnerable or intimidated victims within one working day and all other victims within five working days if there is insufficient evidence to charge a defendant, and identifying any special measures that may be appropriate. For the first time, the Code gives the right to appeal should victims feel that any of the agencies have not met their obligations as set out in the Code.

Compliance with the Code is important but it only formalises many of the good things that the CPS is already doing. The Service is also undertaking a best practice review of Direct Communication with Victims to ensure that it can be confident of meeting the commitments set out in the Victims' Code.

Victim and Witness Care Project: 'No Witness No Justice'

The NWNJ project is a partnership between the Prime Minister's Office of Public Services Reform (OPSR), the CPS, ACPO and OCJR. The initiative aims to provide a more customer-focused and responsive service to victims and witnesses and to improve their experience of the CJS.

NWNJ successfully implemented 165 Witness Care Units (WCUs) in England and Wales by March 2005 to provide an enhanced level of service to all witnesses where a charge has been brought. This includes completing needs assessments, to identify issues such as childcare or travel to and from the court, and organising pre-court familiarisation visits.

Cases handled by WCUs have improved witness attendance rates from 78.5% to 84% and the number of trials that did not go ahead as planned because a witness did not attend has fallen from an average of 908 in a month to 727 in a month, a decrease of 19.9%. During 2006 WCUs will work to achieve the highest standards through the implementation of the 14 'minimum requirements' for providing witness services.

The NWNJ project will continue to rollout the Witness Management IT System used in WCUs to track the progress of cases and help witness care officers provide a comprehensive service to meet the needs of victims and witnesses.

Improving the Service to Vulnerable or Intimidated Witnesses

The CPS continues to work closely with OCJR and other agencies to implement the special measures contained in Part II of the Youth Justice and Criminal Evidence Act 1999. Since October 2005, live links have been available for all vulnerable and intimidated witnesses in both the Crown Court and magistrates' courts. In 2006, the CPS intends to implement video evidence for intimidated witnesses in some categories of crime including rape and serious sexual assault. Six Pathfinder Areas have continued their work on the use of intermediaries for vulnerable witnesses and the evaluation team will report on this in 2006 before deciding on national rollout.

The CPS has also continued its programme of Area events to encourage the use of 'witness profiling' for vulnerable witnesses in partnership with Liverpool City Council. This includes working with Social Services to increase support, including pre-court visits, and identifying possible special measures that a witness may need.

Domestic Violence

The CPS continues to contribute to the Government's strategy to tackle domestic violence. Key elements of the CPS policy on prosecuting cases of domestic violence, which was revised in 2005, included a greater focus on the victim's priorities of safety, support and information and, wherever possible, constructing cases for prosecution on the basis of evidence other than that from the victim.

In June 2005, the CPS completed a two year Domestic Violence Project, with pilots in Caerphilly, Gwent and Croydon. The Project illustrated ways to increase the number of domestic violence incidents reported to police resulting in a case at court; reduce the number of cases withdrawn or discontinued; increase the number of offenders brought to justice, including through more guilty pleas; and strengthen cases through the use of evidence other than victim statements. Good Practice Guidance from this work was distributed to all CPS Areas in November, for use in developing Area Business Plans for 2006-07.

The CPS Domestic Violence Team is also working with the Home Office and DCA to establish 25 specialist domestic violence courts across England and Wales which will be established during 2006-07, and to utilise £2.5 million funding, announced at the end of March 2006, to employ independent domestic violence advisors to support victims in these courts.

Hate Crime

The Attorney General and the DPP launched the CPS Policy on Prosecuting Racist & Religious Crime in July 2003. In 2005-06, CPS reviewed its performance in the prosecution of hate crimes including racist and religious crimes. From April to December 2005 there has been a 33% increase in recorded hate crime cases compared with 2004-05, with domestic violence accounting for over 80% of these cases. From April 2005 targets were introduced to reduce unsuccessful outcomes in hate crimes, with specific reference to domestic violence. From April 2005 to December 2005 hate crime successful outcomes increased from 57.9% to 61.7%, while domestic violence successful outcomes increased from 55% to 59.5%.

Racist Incident Monitoring

The CPS Racist Incident Monitoring Annual Report for the year ending March 2005 was published in November 2005. The number of defendant cases received from the police was 5,788 compared with 4,728 the previous year, an increase of 22.4%. There was sufficient evidence to prosecute in 4666 cases, a 5% increase. The overall conviction rate was 84%.

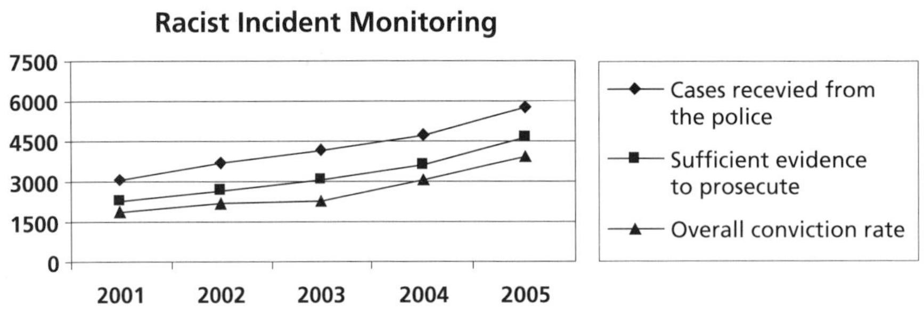

Engaging with Communities

Recovering Proceeds of Crime

From April 2005 to January 2006, the CPS secured 2,447 confiscation orders with a value of over £71 million, exceeding the 2005-06 targets of 2,280 orders to a value of £68 million. The CPS has also obtained 454 restraint orders which is ahead of profile and already exceeds the target for 2005-06 of 431 orders.

The CPS/Enforcement Task Force continues to recover monies in respect of confiscation orders and compensation orders on behalf of victims.

The Regional Asset Recovery Teams have contributed by assisting in obtaining larger value Confiscation Orders and in other areas of asset recovery work such as co-ordinating local training and disseminating best practice.

Tackling Anti-Social Behaviour

During 2005-06, the Anti-Social Behaviour (ASB) Project continued to build on work carried out by the Specialist Prosecutors in 14 CPS Areas. All Areas have negotiated protocols with partner agencies, and carried out extensive training for staff and for colleagues in partner agencies. Action plans on how an Area intends to implement ASB policy are in place in the majority of Areas, with the remainder to be completed in 2006-07.

In 2005 HM Crown Prosecution Service Inspectorate (HMCPSI) produced a report on how the CPS was handling ASB and social impact crime. In response to the seven recommendations in the review, the CPS is implementing an action plan which includes appointing an ASB co-ordinator in all Areas and developing an ASB Strategy document to provide good practice and lessons learnt by ASB Specialists.

Community Engagement

The CPS Community Engagement Strategy was agreed in May 2005. The Strategy sets out the high level policy commitments on equality and diversity, the broad outcomes the CPS is seeking to achieve, and the high level actions and areas for future focus to achieve the commitments. To develop the Strategy the CPS has launched three community engagement pilots to look at different ways of engaging with the wide range of communities. The West Yorkshire pilot is building community engagement into the day-to-day business, focusing on two geographic areas (rural and urban), by providing communities with information about hate crime and a business plan that takes the communities views into account. Thames Valley is looking at innovative ways of engaging local citizens and the business community, in a city centre, a town and a medium sized village, to improve the response to anti-social behaviour at a multi-agency level. Durham is exploring ways of building the confidence of local communities, particularly those affected by hate crime to encourage more people to come forward and remain involved in cases. These pilots will help inform good practice guidance to be issued in 2006-07.

The CPS has introduced an initiative to increase engagement with Muslim communities through a series of meetings in eight Areas in England and Wales during 2006. The first meeting took place in London in February, and consisted of presentations from CPS prosecutors dealing with counter terrorism, incitement to racial hatred, and racially and religiously aggravated crime, and concluded with a discussion on the issues raised.

Improving Communications

The key roles of the Communication Division (CD) are to explain the work of the CPS, thereby helping to improve public confidence in the CJS; to engender a sense of shared purpose among staff, working towards the attainment of the Vision for the CPS; and to assist the flow of information across the Service. It also provides support for communication managers in the CPS Areas. To achieve this the CPS issues and updates leaflets throughout the year on topics such as householders and the use of force against intruders, and the CPS schools video, Just Deserts, is now included in the National Curriculum Citizenship Module.

Following an independent review of CPS communications, the CPS is implementing a programme of strategic communication work. This programme is designed to help improve CPS performance and to increase awareness of the work the CPS is delivering for the public.

Freedom of Information

The Freedom of Information Act 2000 (FOIA) came into full force on 1 January 2005. The Act gives a right of access to anyone to recorded information held by public authorities. During 2005, the CPS received and responded to 378 requests and 29 internal reviews in relation to FOIA, and 69 Data Protection subject access requests. The CPS continues to work towards our legal obligations under the Acts and promote an open and honest culture across the Service.

Driving Change and Delivery

Criminal Case Management

The CPS has been working with the OCJR, other CJS agencies, the senior judiciary and representatives from the defence in the production of the next edition of the Criminal Case Management Framework (CCMF) for hearings involving adults. The CCMF articulates the roles and responsibilities of the agencies in bringing offenders to justice by helping to improve case preparation and progression from charge to finalisation. The CCMF is being implemented through the Effective Trial Management Programme and was introduced in all 42 Areas by March 2006 as part of the overall strategy to reduce the number of ineffective trials in the Crown Court and in magistrates' courts.

Work is currently underway to produce a CCMF for Youth cases. The CPS is again working as part of the multi-agency Case Management Team within the OCJR to assist in the production of the YCCMF by the summer of 2006.

Prolific and Priority Offenders

The CPS has continued to work closely at a national and local level during 2005-06 with Crime and Disorder Reduction Partnerships and Community Safety Groups on the three-strand Prolific and Priority Offender (PPO) Programme. Working predominantly with police partners the CPS has focused on the 'Catch and Convict' strand, providing a premium service in terms of the preparation and presentation of cases involving offenders alleged to represent a significant threat to the wellbeing of the local community.

CJS performance is monitored through J-Track, an IT system used to track and monitor PPOs. A J-Track London User Group has been set up to raise awareness within CPS London of this part of the PPO process and best practice from this group will be promulgated to other Areas.

Drug Intervention Programme

The Drug Intervention Programme (DIP) involves the CPS, criminal justice agencies and the National Treatment Agency working with other service providers to offer a way out for offenders regularly committing crime to fund their drug habit. CPS performance is measured by comparing Home Office figures for the number of drug tests carried out, to the number of DIP cases that have been identified. CPS compliance has risen from 46% in April 2005 to 87% in January 2006. To improve performance further the CPS Priority Offenders Delivery Unit has held four DIP seminars and visited five CPS Areas to look at local systems, discuss issues, and disseminate best practice.

In March 2006, 'Testing on Arrest' and 'Restriction on Bail' provisions came into force to encourage earlier and better levels of drug intervention. Under 'Testing on Arrest' offenders are being tested at arrest instead of at charge, allowing the initial drug assessment to be completed in the police station and increasing the chances of meaningful drug rehabilitation. 'Restriction on Bail' applies across England and makes drug treatment a condition of bail where someone has tested positive for drugs. In preparation for the launch of these two important initiatives the CPS has held three national seminars for staff with invited speakers representing the Home Office, Government Office for London and Metropolitan Police.

Prosecution Team Performance Management

The CPS is working closely with ACPO and individual police forces to complete the implementation of a joint performance management system that will enable the police and CPS to monitor and improve management in cases that are brought for prosecution. Building on the existing CPS Case Management System, the Prosecution Team Performance Management (PTPM) arrangements provide detailed data at police Basic Command Unit level to monitor performance of cases handled both at the pre-charge and post-charge stage. PTPM has been implemented in 41 Areas with the remaining Area to rollout shortly.

Working with the Bar

Since its inception in 1986, the CPS has been a regular purchaser of advocacy services from self-employed barristers to supplement the advocacy provided by in-house Crown Prosecutors in both magistrates' courts and the Crown Court. In 2005, for the first time, some self-employed barristers decided not to accept defence or prosecution work in a dispute over the level of legal aid fees being paid by the DCA. The dispute lasted for about a month during October.

Throughout 2005-06, including during the dispute period, the CPS maintained good relationships with the Bar Council representatives at a national level and with circuit leaders at a local level through the Joint Advocate Selection Committees.

Developing Criminal Justice Information Technology

Working in collaboration with the police and CJIT, the CPS has successfully piloted the electronic transfer of case information between police and CPS IT systems. The CJS Exchange facility, created by CJIT, has enabled immediate electronic information sharing between the CPS and partner agencies. The initial pilot between the CPS Case Management System and police National Strategy in Police Information Systems in Humberside was successfully concluded in 2005 and the exchange is now live in Avon and Somerset. These interfaces will continue to rollout throughout 2006-07. By using the interface, the burden of inputting the same data into both police and CPS systems has been substantially reduced.

The CPS has also worked closely with the DCA and has completed the rollout of the Exchange of Hearing Information By Internet Technology (XHIBIT) which provides up-to-date listing and results information for the CPS and for victims and witnesses at Crown Courts. The CPS continues to work with other prosecuting authorities and with colleagues in the DCA to explore opportunities for making wider use of electronic tools such as electronic presentation of evidence.

Becoming an Employer of Choice

Recruiting and Developing our People

The CPS continues to improve its recruitment procedures. The introduction of the National Recruitment Centre in Liverpool provides both managers and prospective employees with a streamlined and cost efficient service which includes advice from a recruitment professional and an increasing number of vacancies available online. The overall time taken to recruit staff has now reduced to seven weeks. Recruitment initiatives are supported by an induction process, which combines face-to-face training with e-learning through the virtual Prosecution College.

During the last 12 months, the CPS made the following number of appointments on either a permanent or fixed term basis:

CPS Appointments January – December 2005

Level	Total	Female	Ethnic Minority	Appointees who meet the definition of disability under the DDA 1995
Pay Band A1	312	234	8	2
Pay Band A2	249	171	19	0
Pay Band B1	27	21	1	0
Pay Band B2	6	3	0	0
Pay Band B3	5	3	1	0
Pay Band C1	73	49	11	0
Pay Band C2	64	41	18	0
Level D	14	9	2	0
Level E	0	0	0	0
SCS	1	1	0	0
CCP	0	0	0	0
Total	**751**	**532**	**60**	**2**

Figures exclude casuals and temporary members of staff.

Pay Tables

Senior Civil Service (SCS) pay including CCPs and London Sector Directors and Business Managers (SBMs) as at 1st April 2005.

Salary Range	SCS	CCP/SBM	TOTAL
£55,000 – £59,999	1		1
£60,000 – £64,999			0
£65,000 – £69,999	2	1	3
£70,000 – £74,999	7	7	14
£75,000 – £79,999	3	18	21
£80,000 – £84,999	4	11	15
£85,000 – £89,999	3	4	7
£90,000 – £94,999	3	7	10
£95,000 – £99,999	1	4	5
£100,000 – £104,999	1		1
£105,000 – £109,999	2		2
£110,000 – £114,999	1		1
£115,000 – £119,999			0
£120,000 – £124,999	1	1	2
£125,000 – £129,999	1		1
£130,000 – £134,999			0
£135,000 – £139,999			0
£140,000 – £144,999			0
£145,000 – £149,999			0
Total	**30**	**53**	**83**

Leadership and Development

The Leadership and Management Development Programme 'Transform' has continued to provide development opportunities for managers at all levels. Unit Heads (who manage teams of prosecutors, caseworkers, and administration staff in Areas) have participated in a comprehensive leadership development programme, and executive coaching has been undertaken by a cadre of senior managers. Working with the NWNJ project, all Witness Care Managers have completed tailored management training and a number of bespoke development programmes have been delivered for individual management teams.

Law Scholarship Scheme

Since the scheme began in 2003, 549 staff have benefited, or continue to benefit, from the opportunities provided, including 51 Scholars who have qualified as solicitors or barristers. This achievement was recognised in November 2005 when the CPS won the Personnel Today award for Excellence in Training – with the Law Scholarship Scheme and Legal Trainee schemes both forming part of this joint award.

In 2005-06 there were 331 Scholars, including 45 legal trainees. Also this year a national campaign to attract external applicants for the Legal Trainee Scheme was undertaken. A total of 2,219 applications were received for 25 posts.

Representative Workforce

The CPS Annual Equalities in Employment Report 2004-05 was published in January 2006. The report shows a significant increase in the number of senior women employees and the numbers of Black and Minority Ethnic legal trainees in the past year. The number of female CPS employees at Senior Civil Service level has increased to 33.3%, with female CCPs increasing to 24.5%. In April 2005 Black and Minority Ethnic employees made up 14.8% of all CPS employees, exceeding the civil service average of 8.1%.

Equality and Diversity Awards

The CPS received a number of awards in 2005-06 for its work on equality and diversity, including the Commission for Racial Equality – Law Society Race Equality Award for best large public sector employer of solicitors, and the HR Excellence Award on Diversity.

Capability to Deliver

Restructuring

The programme to restructure and professionalise Human Resources (HR) Directorate was completed in 2005. HR Business Partners were introduced to improve performance management, provide strong, professional advice to frontline managers and develop effective HR policies in support of the Service's reform programme.

Following a review of the way it provides support services to Areas and HQ, CPS has rationalised its ten Service Centres into five specialist Business Centres for the provision of Pay, Recruitment, HR Advice, Finance, and Facilities Management. The migration of this work was completed in August 2005, and the next year will be spent implementing revised processes and retraining staff to improve efficiency and customer service. The Service Centre rationalisation is allowing CPS to relocate around 30 posts from the South East and meet commitments in the Lyons Review.

In January 2005 an implementation plan was put in place for Policy Directorate to become more pro-active and outward looking, with the introduction of Account Managers responsible for influencing criminal justice legislation and reform in the Home Office and the DCA. The Business Information Systems Directorate has also streamlined its management team and increased its capability to provide information and communications technology support to the prosecution process; and to work with CJIT, the police and courts to join up CJS IT systems.

Police Reform

The CPS is facing a challenging time in the months ahead as it awaits the Government's final set of decisions on the restructuring of the Police Service. To ensure it retains the benefits that have been derived from working in an aligned structure, the CPS plans to restructure CPS Areas to follow the same geographical boundaries as the new strategic police forces. The CPS aims to move quickly during 2006-07 to end the uncertainty for staff and to create the new CPS Areas as soon as there is a definitive picture of the number and structure of new police force Areas. It is currently intended to bring those new CPS Areas into being in 2007-08.

The CPS also intends to create Casework Units dedicated to serious crime cases in Areas which will mirror the Protective Service Units which are likely to be created in each of the new police forces. In this way, the CPS will ensure that it provides legal advice of the highest calibre at all stages of investigations into serious crime and bring the strongest possible prosecution case to court.

Improving Governance Arrangements

In line with good practice, a review is being undertaken of the effectiveness of the corporate governance arrangements introduced in November 2004. The review is evaluating the extent to which the arrangements comply with HM Treasury's Code of Good Corporate Governance.

Emerging findings suggest that the introduction of a smaller, more strategic decision making Board has been a success. In support of the Board, the CPS has introduced a Committee structure covering: Policy, Strategy and Diversity; Delivery and Change; People and Equality; Information and Communications Technology; Finance; Professional Standards; and Audit. The Board and Committees have significant CCP and ABM involvement and allow an increased role for the CPS's three Non-Executive Directors. This structure complies with the Code of Good Corporate Governance and no major decisions on prosecution policies, new initiatives, human resources, ICT or investment decisions are made without going through the appropriate Committee or Board arrangements.

The review was completed in March 2006 and any required changes in how business is managed within the Governance arrangements will be implemented in 2006-07.

Improving the Management of Prosecution Costs

The CPS works closely with the DCA on a shared strategy for defence and prosecution costs, to ensure that both parts of government are joined-up in their approach to dealing with the management of criminal cases.

A key focus of CPS activity in 2005 has been to improve the management of Very High Cost Cases. There are a small number of such cases but they can have a significant impact on expenditure of prosecution costs. In July 2005, the CPS introduced a new way of procuring the services of barristers in very high cost cases through new contract arrangements in West Yorkshire, Greater Manchester and the former Casework Directorate. The new contract arrangements achieve greater certainty around the fees payable for cases that are due to last eight weeks or more. The contract agrees an hourly rate at the beginning of a case and plans and manages the work of counsel in 8-12 week stages. The Very High Cost Cases contract arrangements will be rolled out across the whole of the Service during 2006.

The CPS also implemented Case Management Panels during 2005. These are high level Panels that require senior management to scrutinise cases before they begin and ensure that a considered prosecution strategy is in place. The most significant Case Management Panels are chaired by the DPP, others are chaired by Chief Crown Prosecutors or Heads of Casework Divisions. The Panels provide assurances to the Attorney, and the wider CJS community, that appropriate consideration has been given to all pertinent issues surrounding the launch of any substantial prosecution case due to last eight weeks or more at trial, and that the case is kept under regular review.

Centre of Excellence

The CPS Project and Programme Management Centre of Excellence (COE) promotes and shares programme and project management knowledge and techniques, spreads understanding of proven methods for successful change management, and helps develop appropriate programme and project management training.

During 2005 the COE, working collaboratively with staff across HQ Directorates, developed a report that provided an overview of the strategic change portfolio for the Delivery and Change Committee; trained staff in project management techniques; designed an e-learning module for project management; managed the OGC Gateway process for CPS projects; and started a programme of health checks for CPS change programmes and projects, including NWNJ, Witness Management System, and the Personnel Information Management System replacement project.

Sustainable Development

The CPS approach to sustainable development is to:

- Integrate sustainable development into decision making;
- Raise awareness of sustainable development; and
- Improve the performance of the estate.

Performance on the social, community and economic aspects of sustainable development are reported on throughout this report: this section concentrates on environmental protection. The Sustainable Development in Government Report identified a number of areas for improvement across government. To address issues raised, the CPS, along with the other Law Officers Departments, has agreed the Law Officers' Departments Sustainable Development Action plan. The plan will raise awareness of sustainable development issues and includes work to conserve energy, minimise waste and ensure buildings are operated to improve environmental performance.

In 2004-05 49.8% of electricity purchased directly by the CPS was from renewable sources and consumption of fossil fuels reduced by 12% compared to 2000-01. The majority of the CPS uses recycled paper.

The Central Property Unit and Procurement and Commercial Services continue to work jointly to ensure that appropriate aspects of sustainable development are included in criteria when evaluating suppliers for the provision of goods and services. Suppliers are actively encouraged to put forward innovative solutions that address sustainable development.

Improved Procurement

In 2005-06 CPS has continued to develop eProcurement to deliver efficiency savings. All requirements over £50,000 were tendered electronically, reducing the cost of conducting the tender process for both the department and suppliers. Online ordering solutions are now available for stationery, printing, hotel accommodation and rail bookings. The CPS has also successfully used framework contracts arranged by other government departments for its requirements in respect of stationery, reprographics, hotel accommodation and conference bookings, temporary staff, professional services, furniture and information network services.

The CPS awarded a significant contract for the provision of telephony services during the year. The new technology available through this contract will provide the opportunity to achieve cost savings and enable the department to consider new and innovative ways of working for staff, including remote working.

The new contract for information network services will provide the CPS with a strategic information management capability enabling the Service to improve the way it stores, manages and disseminates information, both internally and externally to the public and other members of the criminal justice community. The system, Infonet, will also bring improved ability, through electronic document management, for the CPS to meet FOI and Data Protection Act access requests.

Exploiting Modern IT

The COMPASS Programme is a Private Finance Initiative (PFI) between the CPS and LogicaCMG and gives CPS prosecutors, caseworkers and administrators the technology they need to deliver a constantly improving, modern and efficient service to the public.

The COMPASS infrastructure has grown from supporting staff in less than 100 sites in 2001, to supporting staff working in 680 sites, with the added dimension of 1,000 staff having access to our systems from anywhere in the United Kingdom via a telephone line. The number of users, including police staff, has grown by 31% to 8,900; and court links have increased by 300% to 200. Over 100 CPS Direct staff now have IT links to work from home and provide a 24/7 advice service to the police.

Since the implementation of the Case Management System in 2003, approximately 4,000,000 cases have been registered on the system, allowing information to be input and retrieved quickly in support of effective decision making.

Estates Management

The CPS has continued to implement its Estates Management Strategy in order to ensure that the property portfolio is able to meet current and future business requirements; and control and obtain value for money from the costs of accommodation.

The CPS has significantly reduced the amount of surplus and vacant space during the year from 4979 square metres to 1307 square metres. The in-year reduction in vacant space has enabled savings of approximately £480,000 to be released for other initiatives in future years. Projected accommodation cost per head for 2005-06 is £5,220 calculated on a resource accounts basis, compared with £5,196 in 2004-05.

During the year 10 rent reviews were concluded by the managing agents who represent the CPS resulting in rental increases significantly below market trends. The premises affected amount to one third of the CPS rent commitment. Following a competitive tender, the Service has also appointed new mechanical and electrical contractors under incentivised contracts that reflect performance against agreed criteria.

Health and Safety

The CPS has continued with a programme to increase awareness of health and safety across the service. An inaugural 'CPS Health and Safety Day' was held in June with the participation of 62 CPS offices and HMCPSI. The day was organised locally around a general theme of manual handling and involved quizzes and competitions. Minutes of all national groups, such as the Departmental Health and Safety Committee and the Health and Safety Forum, are available on the CPS intranet, along with the Health and Safety Policy Statement, Guidance Manual and other health and safety related documents. This ensures that a wide range of information is easily available to all staff.

Maximising Attendance

The CPS continues to make progress in reducing the level of sickness absence. The most recent government figures published in November 2005 show the CPS absence rate at 8.7 days, which is 4.5% below the civil service average. The CPS has reviewed its policies and ensured that sufficient support is in place through the introduction of a new counselling and support service. In 2006-07 the CPS will promote the physical, mental and social wellbeing of staff. Through the use of occupational health services in partnership with managers, the CPS will focus on the effect of work on health as well as the effect of health on work. The CPS will also be providing support through stress counselling and promoting healthy lifestyles to avoid sick absence and will also provide support to those who are off sick in order to secure an early return to work.

Forward Look

The CPS is transforming itself into a world-class prosecuting authority and valued public service through its challenging reform program. An effective CJS must have at its centre a strong, confident and independent CPS playing a full part in wider ranging CJS reforms. This will demand hard work and commitment and a continued passion for justice, public service and excellence from all CPS people and will test to the full the Service's ability as an organisation to adapt and learn to become a strong confident CPS.

The CPS is developing a more flexible and responsive approach to prosecuting different types of crime and criminality, from dealing with anti-social behaviour, hate crimes and domestic violence to tackling serious and organised crime and terrorism, and recovering assets from criminals. It is also becoming more accountable to the public for the quality of the service it delivers and the decisions that prosecutors make every day. Building links with the communities it serves, responding to concerns and making communities safer places to live.

The CPS will continue to develop its role in a more effective and efficient CJS and work for the next year is outlined in the CPS Business Plan 2006-07.

Further Information

More information on the CPS, its contribution to PSA targets and CJS reform, and its modernisation plans is available at www.cps.gov.uk and from:

Crown Prosecution Service
50 Ludgate Hill
London EC4M 7EX

Telephone: 0207 796 8000

Bibliography

2004-2005 Annual Report for the Crown Prosecution Service
Resource Estimates 2005-2006: The Crown Prosecution Service
The Code for Crown Prosecutors – available at the CPS website:
http://www.cps.gov.uk/victims_witnesses/code.html

*Spending 2002 & 2004
*Special Delivery Agreements
*Public Service Agreements
*Departmental Investment Strategy

*available at the Treasury web site:

http://www.hm-treasury.gov.uk/spending_review/spend_sr02/spend_sr02_index.cfm
http://www.hm-treasury.gov.uk/spending_review/spend_sr04/spend_sr04_index.cfm
http://www.hm-treasury.gov.uk/performance/

Common Core Tables

Total public spending for The Crown Prosecution Service £'000

	2000-01 Outturn	2001-02 Outturn	2002-03 Outturn	2003-04 Outturn	2004-05 Outturn	2005-06 Esimated Outturn	2006-07 Plans	2007-08 Plans
Consumption of resources:								
Increase public confidence in the Criminal Justice System through fair, firm and effective prosecutions.	338,342	405,868	451,293	512,517	565,363	603,434	599,880	632,075
Total resource budget	**338,342**	**405,868**	**451,293**	**512,517**	**565,363**	**603,434**	**599,880**	**632,075**
of which:								
Resource DEL [1 & 2]	338,342	405,868	451,293	512,517	565,363	603,434	599,880	632,075
Capital spending:								
Increase public confidence in the Criminal Justice System through fair, firm and effective prosecutions.	12,984	21,340	5,528	7,370	7,042	5,000	7,400	7,400
Total capital budget	**12,984**	**21,340**	**5,528**	**7,370**	**7,042**	**5,000**	**7,400**	**7,400**
of which:								
Capital DEL [2]	12,984	21,340	5,528	7,370	7,042	5,000	7,400	7,400
Total public spending [1 & 2]	**346,372**	**397,445**	**454,919**	**517,535**	**569,041**	**604,878**	**602,224**	**634,419**

(1) Departmental Expenditure Limits, set as part of the 2004 Spending Review.
(2) Total public spending calculated as the total of the resource budget plus the capital budget, less depreciation and impairment.

Crown Prosecution Service: Capital Employed £'000

	2000-01 Outturn	2001-02 Outturn	2002-03 Outturn	2003-04 Outturn	2004-05 Outturn	2005-06 Forecast	2006-07 Projected	2007-08 Projected
Assets on balance sheet at end of the year:								
Fixed Assets	19,874	12,094	15,678	20,898	27,735	19,696	21,361	23,026
Intangible	0	0	0	0	0	894	745	596
Tangible								
of which:								
Land and buildings	3,901	3,903	3,564	3,378	5,775	5,365	5,179	4,993
Plant and machinery	15,973	8,191	12,114	17,520	21,960	13,437	15,437	17,437
Investments								
Current Assets	40,423	66,364	61,156	50,839	76,164	28,457	29,026	29,607
Creditors (<1 year)	–30,627	–63,478	–68,588	–53,273	–82,343	–21,715	–22,149	–22,592
Creditors (>1 year)	–	–	–	–	–		–	–
Provisions	–8,460	–13,055	–12,112	–11,467	–11,075	–9,759	–7,589	–5,809
Capital employed within main department	**21,210**	**1,925**	**–3,866**	**6,997**	**10,481**	**16,679**	**20,649**	**24,231**
NDPB net assets	–	–	–	–	–	0	0	0
Total capital employed in departmental group	**21,210**	**1,925**	**–3,866**	**6,997**	**10,481**	**16,679**	**20,649**	**24,231**

Administration costs for the Crown Prosecution Service £'000

	2000-01 Outturn	2001-02 Outturn	2002-03 Outturn	2003-04 Outturn	2004-05 Outturn	2005-06 Estimated Outturn	2006-07 Plans	2007-08 Plans
Gross administration costs:								
Other[1]	16,000	17,493	16,669	20,998	26,421	29,220	–	–
Paybill	20,671	24,836	27,574	32,357	32,282	24,000	–	–
Total gross administration costs	**36,671**	**42,329**	**44,243**	**53,355**	**58,703**	**53,220**	**58,353**	**58,353**
Related administration cost receipts[2]	–1,834	–2,146	–2,354	–2,570	–1,256	–300	–400	–400
Total net administration costs								
Analysis by activity:								
Increase confidence in the criminal justice system through fair, firm and effective prosecutions	34,837	40,183	41,889	50,785	57,447	52,920	57,953	57,953
Total net administration costs								
Controls and limits:	**34,837**	**40,183**	**41,889**	**50,785**	**57,447**	**52,920**	**57,953**	**57,953**
Administration costs limits (net) for gross controlled areas:								
The Crown Prosecution Service	34,837	40,183	41,889	50,785	57,447	52,920	57,953	57,953
Total net limits for gross controlled areas	**34,837**	**40,183**	**41,889**	**50,785**	**57,447**	**52,920**	**57,953**	**57,953**

[1] 2001-02 includes £22 million exceptional impairment costs from the transfer of IT assets.

[2] Decrease in administration cost receipts from 2005-06 onwards is due to the review of administration costs.

Staff Numbers Staff-Years

	2000-01 Actual	2001-02 Actual	2002-03 Actual	2003-04 Actual	2004-05 Actual	2005-06 Estimated	2006-07 Plans	2007-08 Plans
Crown Prosecution Service:								
CS FTEs	5,564	6,240	6,680	7,257	7,555	7,846	8,084	8,194
Overtime	44	40	41	49	38	41	45	50
Casuals	211	270	313	357	282	129	53	50
Total	**5,819**	**6,550**	**7,034**	**7,663**	**7,875**	**8,016**	**8,182**	**8,294**

The Crown Prosecution Service's identifiable expenditure on services, by country and region — £ million

	2000-01 Outturn	2001-02 Outturn	2002-03 Outturn	2003-04 Outturn	2004-05 Plans	2005-06 Plans	2006-07 Plans	2007-08 Plans
North East	18.7	21.6	24.2	28.6	29.2	32.0	32.9	34.5
North West	54.0	59.8	68.9	78.2	86.9	92.3	92.7	97.1
Yorkshire and Humberside	33.7	36.8	43.4	49.0	54.7	54.9	57.1	59.8
East Midlands	24.3	28.3	31.0	35.6	38.2	41.5	42.2	44.2
West Midlands	33.3	38.5	44.5	52.4	58.5	62.4	61.1	64.0
Eastern	28.0	31.1	35.7	40.4	42.8	45.9	47.3	49.5
London	63.3	76.8	96.8	110.3	124.8	129.0	124.5	130.1
South East	40.7	45.1	53.4	60.4	64.3	67.9	69.4	72.5
South West	25.8	27.2	29.5	33.4	37.4	39.1	40.2	42.3
Total England	**321.8**	**365.2**	**427.4**	**488.3**	**536.8**	**565.0**	**567.4**	**594.0**
Scotland	0.0	0.0	0.0	0.0	0.0	0.0	0.0	0.0
Wales	24.3	26.7	27.8	29.8	31.6	35.0	36.8	38.6
Northern Ireland	0.0	0.0	0.0	0.0	0.0	0.0	0.0	0.0
Total UK identifiable expenditure	**346.1**	**391.9**	**455.2**	**518.1**	**568.4**	**600.0**	**604.2**	**632.6**
Outside UK	0.0	0.0	0.0	0.0	0.0	0.0	0.0	0.0
Total identifiable expenditure	**346.1**	**391.9**	**455.2**	**518.1**	**568.4**	**600.0**	**604.2**	**632.6**
Non-identifiable expenditure	0.0	0.0	0.0	0.0	0.0	0.0	0.0	0.0
Total expenditure on services	**346.1**	**391.9**	**455.2**	**518.1**	**568.4**	**600.0**	**604.2**	**632.6**

The Crown Prosecution Service's identifiable expenditure on services, by country and region, per head — £'s per head

	2000-01 Outturn	2001-02 Outturn	2002-03 Outturn	2003-04 Outturn	2004-05 Plans	2005-06 Plans	2006-07 Plans	2007-08 Plans
North East	7.4	8.5	9.5	11.3	11.5	12.6	13.0	13.7
North West	8.0	8.8	10.2	11.5	12.7	13.5	13.6	14.2
Yorkshire and Humberside	6.8	7.4	8.7	9.8	10.9	10.9	11.3	11.8
East Midlands	5.8	6.8	7.3	8.4	8.9	9.7	9.8	10.2
West Midlands	6.3	7.3	8.4	9.8	11.0	11.7	11.4	11.9
Eastern	5.2	5.8	6.6	7.4	7.8	8.3	8.5	8.8
London	8.7	10.5	13.1	14.9	16.8	17.3	16.6	17.2
South East	5.1	5.6	6.6	7.5	7.9	8.3	8.5	8.8
South West	5.2	5.5	5.9	6.7	7.4	7.7	7.9	8.2
Total England	**6.5**	**7.4**	**8.6**	**9.8**	**10.7**	**11.2**	**11.2**	**11.7**
Scotland	0.0	0.0	0.0	0.0	0.0	0.0	0.0	0.0
Wales	8.4	9.2	9.5	10.1	10.7	11.8	12.3	12.9
Northern Ireland	0.0	0.0	0.0	0.0	0.0	0.0	0.0	0.0
Total UK identifiable expenditure	**5.9**	**6.6**	**7.7**	**8.7**	**9.5**	**10.0**	**10.0**	**10.5**

- The spending data shown in these tables is consistent with the country and regional analyses (CRA) published by HM Treasury in chapter 7 of Public Expenditure Statistical Analyses (PESA) 2006. PESA contains more tables analysed by country and region, and also explains how the analysis was collected and the basis for allocating expenditure between countries and regions.
- The tables include the spending of the department and its NDPBs on payments to private sector and subsidies to public corporations. They do not include capital finance to public corporations but do include public corporations capital expenditure. They do not include payments to local authorities or local authorities own expenditure.
- The data are based on a subset of spending – identifiable expenditure on services – which is capable of being analysed as being for the benefit of individual countries and regions. Expenditure that is incurred for the benefit of the UK as a whole is excluded.
- The tables do not include depreciation, cost of capital charges or movements in provisions that are in DEL/AME. They do include salaries, procurement expenditure, capital expenditure and grants and subsidies paid to individuals and private sector enterprises.
- The figures were taken from the HM Treasury Public spending database in December 2005 and the regional distributions were completed in January/February 2006. Therefore the tables may not show the latest position and are not consistent with other tables in the Department report.
- Across government, most expenditure is not planned or allocated on a regional basis. Social security payments, for example, are paid to eligible individuals irrespective of where they live. Expenditure on other programmes is allocated by looking at how all the projects across the departments area of responsibility, usually England, compare. So the analysis shows the regional outcome of spending decisions that have on the whole not been made primarily on a regional basis.
- The functional categories used are the standard United Nations Classifications of the Functions of Government (COFOG) categories. This is not the same as the strategic priorities used elsewhere in the report.

2 Revenue and Customs Prosecutions Office

REVENUE and CUSTOMS PROSECUTIONS OFFICE

Introduction

Customs and Excise prosecutions have been the subject of a number of reviews in recent years.

The Gower Hammond Review considered the structure and practices of the Prosecutions Group within the Customs and Excise Solicitors Office, and in April 2002 it recommended that the Group should be given greater autonomy within the Solicitor's Office. In response to this recommendation the Prosecutions Group became accountable to the Attorney General for casework decisions. It was also given its own ring-fenced budget and renamed the Customs and Excise Prosecutions Office (CEPO).

In July 2003, the Butterfield Report recommended a complete separation of the prosecution function for Customs and Excise criminal cases from the organisation itself, through the creation of a separate prosecuting authority. The Attorney General announced in October 2004 that Inland Revenue prosecutions would join this new independent prosecuting authority, in line with the merger of the functions of Customs and Excise and the Inland Revenue. This new authority would be known as the Revenue and Customs Prosecutions Office (RCPO).

Following the necessary legislative change, the RCPO was created by statute on 18 April 2005.

Role

RCPO is responsible for carrying out criminal prosecutions for Her Majesty's Revenue and Customs (HMRC) and, from 1 April 2006, will play a vital role alongside the CPS in prosecuting cases investigated by the Serious Organised Crime Agency (SOCA).

RCPO provides a fair, effective and independent prosecution service by:

- Advising HMRC and SOCA on possible prosecutions and other legal issues arising during investigations;
- Reviewing cases submitted by HMRC and SOCA, for evidential sufficiency and public interest;
- Preparing cases for court;
- Prosecuting cases at magistrates' courts;
- Prosecuting cases in Crown Courts and higher courts where appropriate;
- Instructing counsel to prosecute cases in Crown Courts and higher courts;
- Working with other agencies to make the Criminal Justice System (CJS) more efficient and effective.

As a major Crown Court prosecutor, RCPO is second only to the Crown Prosecution Service (CPS) in the number of serious cases it handles. In addition, it prosecutes a significant number of cases in the magistrates' courts. RCPO's prosecutions include many large and complex cases involving drugs, alcohol and tobacco smuggling, income tax and other types of large-scale tax fraud, money laundering, export control and sanctions violations.

These are offences that directly impact on the fabric of society, perpetuating the misery of drugs on the streets and depriving our public services of money. By prosecuting the cases efficiently, effectively and in accordance with the Code for Crown Prosecutors[3], the RCPO plays an integral and important role in delivering key elements of the Governments' objectives of protecting tax revenues, tackling drugs and recovering the proceeds of crime.

Organisation

The Attorney General appointed David Green QC to be the first Director of the RCPO, with responsibility for leading the Department's prosecution activity, managing all legal issues, and determining policy. He heads an organisation of approximately 250 staff which includes lawyers, caseworkers and administrators, who are based in London and Manchester. The Director has appointed a Chief Operating Officer, Dave Partridge, to oversee the range of business services required by the RCPO, such as human resources, finance, information systems and the business change programme.

There are five casework divisions reporting to the Director. While multifunctional in capability, they can each be identified by a lead activity. They are:

Division A (Direct Tax)

Division B (Commercial)

Division C (Border Detections)

Division D (Duty and Excise)

Division E (Serious and Organised Crime)

The International, Policy and Advisory Division, headed by Kristin Jones, provides the Director with support on policy and internal quality assurance, while the Asset Forfeiture Unit, headed by Soumya Majumdar, deals with the restraint of proceeds.

[3] See page 12.

Senior Management Structure

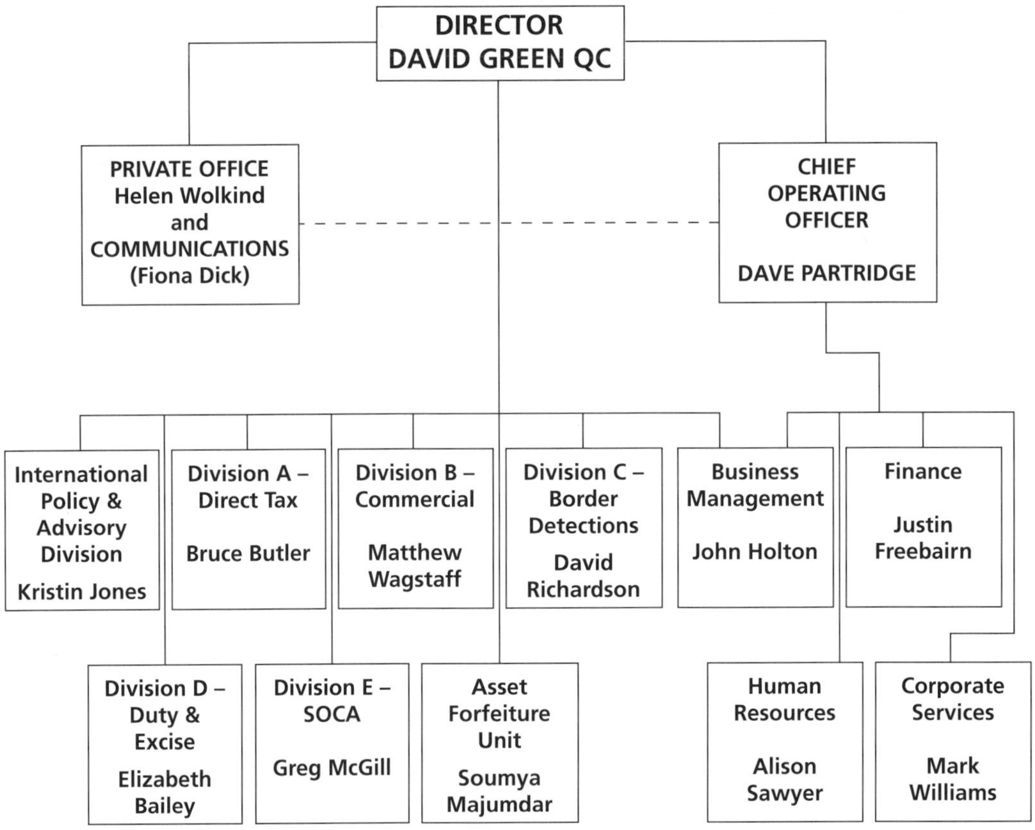

The Director heads a Management Board that includes two non-executive directors, as well as senior members of the organisation. An Audit and Risk Committee, chaired by one of the non-executive directors, assists the Director and the Management Board in fulfilling their oversight responsibilities.

Aim

The RCPO's aim is the delivery of a world-class prosecutions service that commands public and judicial confidence, and plays a major part in the CJS, by:

- Strengthening the prosecution process – bringing more offenders to justice and recovering proceeds of crime;
- Making the RCPO an organisation which is an integral, independent part of the CJS, has the respect of the judiciary and in which there is public confidence. It will do this by acting in accordance with its core values of integrity, professionalism and fairness;
- Driving and responding innovatively and flexibly to change; and
- Effective management of the organisation.

Objectives

As the prosecuting authority for HMRC, the RCPO also supports HMRC in delivery of two of its top-level objectives. These are:

- To improve the extent to which individuals and businesses pay the tax due; and
- Receive the credits and payments to which they are entitled.

To strengthen frontier protection against threats to the security, economic integrity and environment of the United Kingdom in a way that balances the need to maintain the UK as a competitive location in which to do business.

Targets

RCPO contributes towards the CJS PSA[4] targets. The RCPO Business Plan for 2005-06 contains a range of key performance measures that enables the Department to monitor its operational effectiveness in relation to these targets and to HMRC's objectives above. To 31st March 2005, RCPO was on course to meet its key targets; for example, the department had attended over 70% of its key Crown Court hearings, and defendants had entered guilty pleas in over 60% of cases prosecuted.

Efficiency Delivery Plan

The RCPO has a target to reduce its workforce by 10 years over the baseline figure from 2003-04, and this saving has already been achieved. Also within the time frame of the SR2004 settlement the RCPO has Efficiency Delivery targets to make cashable savings of £2.17 million. Savings in productive time and procurement are the main focus for these cash deliverables. Several projects were started in RCPO's first year, including the phased expansion of the advocacy unit, and they are forecast to start producing efficiency savings from 2006 onwards. Technical notes have been produced that set out the methods and measures that are being used to achieve these savings.

RCPO Performance

People

As at 31 December 2005, the RCPO employed 241 people, including 80 lawyers. 212 members of staff are based in RCPO Headquarters in New Kings Beam House, London. The remaining 29 staff, who comprise Casework Division D, are based in Ralli Quays, Manchester.

---

[4] See page 16.

Workload

From April to December 2005 RCPO prosecuted 1,492 cases, of which guilty pleas were recorded in 1,130 cases (76%). At 31 December the department had 1,146 cases on hand.

Case Outcomes

In the magistrates' courts, guilty pleas have been recorded for 80% of defendants. In the Crown Court, 38% of defendants pleaded guilty. The full remit of casework covers a wide range including:

- VAT fraud – from the simplest repayment fraud to complex cases involving multiple traders;
- Direct tax fraud – from large and sophisticated evasion cases on an international scale to less complex shadow economy frauds;
- Tax credit frauds;
- Excise frauds – tobacco, alcohol and fuels;
- Drug smuggling of all kinds, from those carrying goods on or in their person to massive quantities of Class A drugs smuggled by air or sea;
- Money laundering – generally involving the proceeds of fraud or drugs trafficking;
- UN sanctions cases – these usually involve exports to embargoed destinations or export of military or dual use goods;
- Exotic goods – from conflict diamonds to trafficking in endangered species governed by the Convention on International Trade in Endangered Species (CITES);
- Restraint, confiscation and enforcement proceedings undertaken by the Asset Forfeiture Unit.

RCPO's Funding

RCPO's resources have been provided in line with the 2004 Spending Review. Prior to April 2005, funding for the CEPO was provided by a separate Request for Resource on the Main Estimate for HM Customs and Excise. In 2005-06, the creation of the RCPO has led to the consolidation of this budget with those of the ex-Customs' Asset Forfeiture Unit, and of the ex-IR Crime Group. The Department's estimated expenditure in 2005-06 is £37,885,000, which consists of £19,412,000 for the Administration budget, and £18,473,000 for Programme Costs. In turn, the Administration budget is split between a paybill estimate of £11,738,000 (including a dowry of £350,000 from HMRC) and other costs totalling £7,674,000 (including a dowry of £400,000).

Regulatory Impact Assessment

The RCPO is not a regulatory department but does contribute to Home Office impact assessments on criminal justice legislation and DCA impact assessments when appropriate.

Establishing the Department

The RCPO was established to provide an independent prosecuting authority, separate from the investigation function. Independence from investigators is fundamental to the reputation of RCPO prosecutors and a key constitutional safeguard. Prosecutors continue to work closely with investigation colleagues, building strong cases and delivering robust prosecutions. However, there is independence and transparent accountability on prosecution decisions, with a clear distinction made between the roles and responsibilities of investigators and prosecutors and a clear reporting structure to the Attorney General.

Strengthening the Prosecution Process

The RCPO has introduced a Prosecution Manual which sets standards that allow for the timely service of documents on courts and defence that are complete and accurately assembled, and contributes to CJS initiatives to reduce delay and ineffective hearings. It is intended to provide comprehensive procedural guidance so that staff have the confidence to manage and prosecute cases effectively. Assurance activity is in place to ensure best practice, which is monitored by a Best Practice Group of senior case managers.

A Memorandum of Understanding setting out the relationship between RCPO and HMRC was signed on 18 April 2005. Annexes to the Memorandum in the form of agreements covering Policy and Strategy, Casework Standards and Disclosure have been approved by Ministers and form the basis of the day-to-day interface between the departments. There is regular structured liaison on these issues.

Championing Victims and Witnesses

As the prosecuting authority for HMRC and SOCA, RCPO prosecutions underpin revenue collection and enforcement activity of these two organisations. The "victim" in RCPO casework is the taxpayer and society as a whole, for example, people who are exploited by drug dealers or who suffer from drugs related crime. Witnesses in RCPO cases are mainly investigators who give evidence as part of their jobs, but also includes people in the financial industry, such as accountants, bank employees and employees of money service bureaus.

Engaging with Communities

The key community for RCPO is the wider public rather than specific local communities, and RCPO's community engagement is therefore through support of HMRC initiatives. However, in both the way we prosecute our cases and in our employment systems, RCPO aims to eliminate unlawful discrimination and promote equality of opportunity and good relations between persons of different racial groups.

Building Strong Partnerships

SOCA: RCPO has put in place a fully staffed and trained Division to deliver an effective prosecution service for SOCA from 1 April 2006.

Becoming an Employer of Choice

Advocacy Unit: The Advocacy Unit enables RCPO's in-house advocates to cover preliminary hearings in the Crown Court at our two main court centres, Isleworth and Croydon Crown Court. This year has seen a phased expansion of the Unit as a means of enhancing the opportunities available to RCPO lawyers and gaining recognition for our new Department.

The expansion ensures that RCPO in-house advocates cover all preliminary hearings on Thursday list days and also on some of the other regular list days at Isleworth and Croydon Crown Court. The range of work undertaken includes Plea and Case Management Hearings, Mentions, Sentences and some contested Newton and Confiscation Hearings in our "Fast Track" cases at these court centres. In due course it is hoped to extend the work to cover short trials.

Rights of Audience in the Magistrates' Courts: The Commissioners for Revenue and Customs Act 2005 (CRCA 2005) removed the power of HMRC officers to appear as advocates in the magistrates' courts. This implemented a recommendation of the Gower Hammond Review of December 2000. RCPO took over responsibility for these hearings in April 2005.

Capability to Deliver

Designated Court Centres: RCPO has a national remit but operates from 2 locations in London and Manchester. Its casework is overwhelmingly dealt with in the Crown Court. Major cases are complex and require a large amount of court time. Historically, RCPO has found it difficult to provide the level of cover for trials in the Crown Court that it would wish due to the geographical spread of work. RCPO has therefore commenced a project, working with DCA and the Courts Service, aimed at reducing the number of court centres.

Operating Model Project: The merger of the former IR Crime Group, the former CEPO and part of the former HMC&E Asset Forfeiture Unit (AFU) to form RCPO has necessitated a number of changes. The project has developed a single operating model for HMRC casework, including a single prosecution process with common policies and procedures. The new prosecution process came into effect from 16 January 2006. Where appropriate, consequential organisational, structural and management changes have been made.

Disclosure of material: RCPO recognises that it is essential that its disclosure obligations are properly discharged in all criminal proceedings. The Department has delivered extensive training and guidance during the past year to support a regime that follows the Attorney General's Guidelines on Disclosure 2005. There are regular meetings between HMRC and RCPO to ensure that there is effective revelation and disclosure in RCPO.

Accommodation: In response to the recommendations made by the Gower Hammond and Butterfield Reports, RCPO is in the process of implementing an accommodation improvement programme. The programme will improve the workspace for legal staff by bringing about a quieter environment and one that is more conducive to legal work. Improvements will also be made to storage as well as case preparation facilities.

Information Services: RCPO are continuing to receive IS services from HMRC and their third party providers (Fujitsu and CapGemini/ASPIRE). During the last 12 months a programme of work has resulted in the successful establishment of IS systems to support RCPO as an independent department. The programme has also supported the integration of processes and procedures previously employed by the CEPO and the IR Crime Group. More recently a second programme of work has commenced. The first phase of which has identified the procurement options available to RCPO in order for it realise wide ranging improvements in the IS services it receives.

Sustainable Development

The RCPO has contributed to the Government's Sustainable Development policies by;

- Working with its partner Departments in the Law Officers Group to share best practice as well as our estates services providers (HMRC and Mapeley);
- Establishing systems to monitor the RCPO's impact on the environment in order to set 2005-06 as the baseline year for future continual improvement targets, against which performance can be measured and monitored.

RCPO will gain the benefit of measures that HMRC and its estates partners are introducing to improve their environmental performance. These include:

- Conserving energy, water, paper and other resources, whilst providing a comfortable working environment;
- Contributing to reduce carbon dioxide emissions by 12.5 per cent by 2010-11 relative to 1999-00 through increasing energy efficiency of the buildings we occupy by 15 per cent by 2010-11 relative to 1999-00;
- Reducing waste through reduction, re-use and recycling; reducing the waste going to landfill;
- Reducing water consumption to $7.7m^3$ per year ($7.0m^3$ for new builds and refurbishment works);
- Phasing out ozone depleting and other hazardous substances and those with a high global warming potential.

Further Information

Further information on the work of the RCPO may be obtained from:

Revenue and Customs Prosecutions Office
New Kings Beam House
22 Upper Ground
London SE1 9PJ

Telephone number: 0207 865 5666
Fax: 0870 785 8341
Website: www.rcpo.gov.uk

3

Serious Fraud Office

Serious Fraud Office Tables

SERIOUS FRAUD OFFICE

Introduction

The Serious Fraud Office (SFO) was established by the Criminal Justice Act 1987, following the 1986 Roskill Report. Under that Act its role is to investigate and prosecute cases of serious or complex fraud in England, Wales and Northern Ireland and thus contribute to deterring such fraud. The SFO is headed by the Director, Robert Wardle, who acts under the superintendence of the Attorney General.

In exercising his statutory responsibilities under the Criminal Justice Act 1987, the Director is supported by the Strategic Board and the Operational Board. The Strategic Board comprises the Director, three Non-Executive directors, the Deputy Director, the Head of Resources and Planning, the Head of Policy and the Head of Accountancy. The Operational Board comprises members of the Strategic Board and the five Assistant Directors in charge of operational divisions.

Management Structure

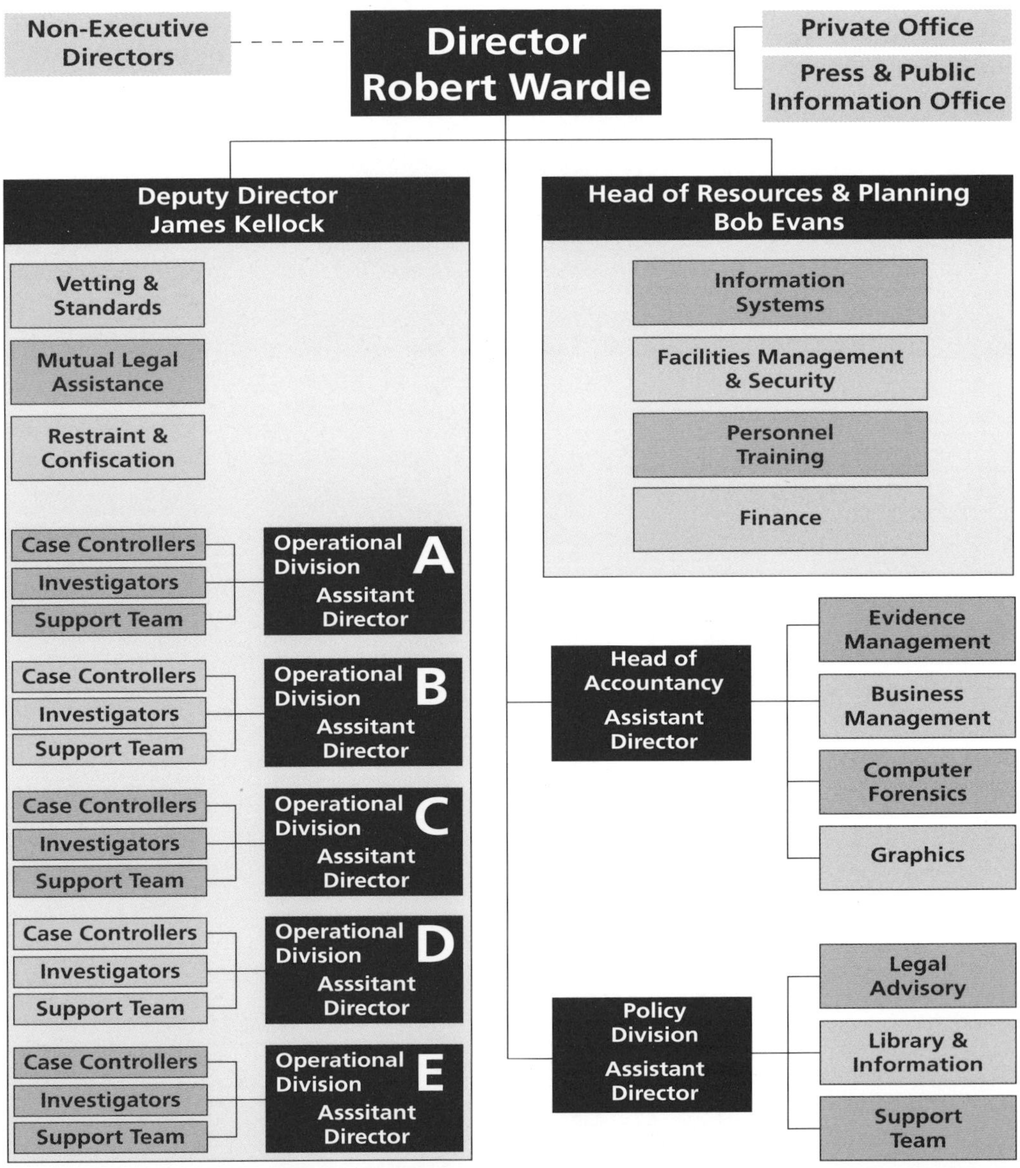

The SFO is part of the Criminal Justice System (CJS) and is affected by changes and developments in that system. To achieve its aim and objectives it must take into account and be part of developments in the wider world of law enforcement and financial regulation.

SFO Performance

Aims and Objectives

Since the SFO became operational in 1988 and to 31 March 2006, 303 trials have taken place resulting in at least one person at a trial being convicted on 241 occasions (80%). These trials involved 663 defendants of whom 458 were convicted (69%). For the period 1 April 2005 to 31 March 2006 there were 10 trials involving 23 defendants completed, of whom 13 were convicted (57%).

The aim of the Serious Fraud Office is to contribute to:

- Reducing fraud and the cost of fraud;
- The delivery of justice and the rule of law; and
- Maintaining confidence in the UK's business and financial institutions.

The objectives of the SFO are to take on appropriate cases and:

- Investigate them and bring them to a successful conclusion as quickly as individual circumstances allow; and
- When a decision to prosecute is made, to prosecute fairly and in a way that enables the jury to understand the issues.

In carrying out its aims and objectives, the SFO will:

- Work effectively and efficiently;
- Co-operate with other agencies and overseas jurisdictions; and
- Ensure that its activities, and the way they are reported, contribute to deterring fraud.

Targets

The key targets to be achieved in 2005-06 were:

- Seek to achieve reductions in investigation and prosecution times for cases; and
- Maintain a caseload of 85 active cases (including appeals) within allocated resources. The caseload at 31 March 2006 was 97.

Additionally the following baseline measure is reported on:

- The long run rate showing defendants successfully prosecuted. This provides a quality check over time. The current long-run rate is 69%; the figure at 2004-05 was 69%. Although there is no 'right' long run rate, a reasonable expectation based on past performance is in the 60-75% range.

Strengthening the Prosecution Process

The SFO is committed to reduce the length of investigation and prosecution phases by being more effective in those areas which it can more closely control. These include:

- Rigorous vetting of cases referred to the Office;
- Terminating investigations which are not likely to lead to a prosecution as quickly as possible;
- Focussing the investigation on key offenders and key charges to avoid over-burdening the investigation and prosecution;
- Transferring cases as quickly as possible to the Crown Court;
- Ensuring cases are presented fairly, concisely and understandably; and continuously improving value for money;
- Using document management systems and information technology to speed up investigations and prosecution; and
- Collaboration and joined up working with partners within the CJS.

The statutory criteria for accepting cases are interpreted in the light of published criteria agreed by the Law Officers. The key criterion for the SFO to take on a case is that the suspected fraud was such that the direction of the investigation should be in the hands of those who will be responsible for the prosecution.

The factors that would need to be taken into account include:

- The sum at risk is estimated to be at least £1 million. (This is simply an objective and recognisable mark of seriousness and likely public concern, rather than the main indicator of suitability);
- The case is likely to give rise to national publicity and widespread public concern. Such cases include those involving government departments, public bodies, the governments of other countries and commercial cases of public interest;
- The case requires a highly specialist knowledge of, for example, financial markets and their practices;
- The case has a significant international dimension;
- There is a need for legal, accountancy, and investigative skills to be brought together;
- The suspected fraud appears to be complex and one in which the use of section two powers (Criminal Justice Act 1987) might be appropriate.

None of those factors, taken individually, would necessarily be regarded as conclusive.

The SFO already deals with money laundering offences arising out of investigations into serious and complex fraud, and is able to investigate any offence which involves such fraud. Offences such as laundering and corruption feature in both current investigations and past prosecutions. The Enterprise Act 2002 criminalised anti-competitive behaviour by individuals and the SFO shares responsibility with OFT for the conduct of criminal prosecutions under this legislation. The Anti-Terrorism, Crime and Security Act 2001 clarified the law relating to the bribery of foreign officials by UK nationals or companies. The SFO has taken responsibility for the initial review of all allegations received in this area. Where sufficient evidence exists we will expect to begin an investigation. If the case should not for some reason fall within our criteria, then we will endeavour to ensure that it is still dealt with by another law enforcement or regulatory body. In order to meet additional responsibilities such as maintaining the register of complaints of suspicion of corruption overseas and an increasing number of applications to restrain the proceeds of crime the SFO has established two small units specialising in these areas.

Building Strong Partnerships

The SFO and the City of London Police Economic Crime Department have built on the initiatives to enable closer collaboration and mutual understanding to tackle fraud within London and the South East. Joint working discussions focussing on effectiveness, efficiency and logistics to support change have continued and positive advances have been made. The development of a joint mobile forensic laboratory capability to enable computer-based material to be accessed at the scene of a search rather than having to remove the hardware to a remote laboratory will allow the computer owner to have his equipment returned more quickly and will make the material available to investigators in a much shorter time.

In London the SFO works primarily with the lead force the City of London Police. A Memorandum of Understanding (MOU) with the Association of Chief Police Officers (ACPO) sets out the agreed approach to SFO investigations, and who will be responsible for different aspects of the work. Each operational division has an alignment with police forces in an operational area although all take cases from the Metropolitan and City police forces. The Police Force Structures Review and proposed consolidation of individual forces may have a significant impact on resources, relationships and the way we work.

A case may be referred to the SFO by the police, the Department of Trade and Industry, another government body or regulator, or sometimes by a liquidator or other statutory office holder. Each is now considered by the Vetting Team and an Assistant Director to decide whether it fulfils the statutory criteria for acceptance. In some cases a preliminary investigation is conducted to establish whether the case will come within the criteria and whether there is a realistic prospect of the investigation resulting in a prosecution. Early referral of cases is encouraged. The SFO is a member of the Joint Vetting Committee (JVC) which includes representatives from a number of organisations in the CJS. Its purpose is to decide which is the most appropriate body to investigate a suspected fraud. To reflect the changes brought about by the creation of the Financial Services Authority (FSA) and Assets Recovery Agency (ARA), the committee has been expanded to include representatives from these organisations. In addition the committee includes representatives from the CPS, Metropolitan Police, City of London Police, ACPO (on behalf of the other police forces), OFT, HM Revenue and Customs and the DTI (investigations branch). The JVC is also a forum for discussing matters of mutual interest.

Working with Bodies Overseas

The SFO has a small unit of investigators dealing exclusively with mutual legal assistance work. The unit is advised by a senior lawyer and assisted by forensic investigators when necessary. During the year assistance was given to 23 countries in the investigation of their cases. These include Israel, South Africa, Zambia, India, Hong Kong, Mexico, USA, St Vincent and the Grenadines and Australia. European countries continue to provide the largest number of requests to the unit with requests from Germany, Italy, Czech Republic, France, The Netherlands, Latvia and Switzerland.

MLA activity

	1999-00	**2000-01**	**2001-02**	**2002-03**	**2003-04**	**2004-05**	**2005–06 (1 Feb)**
Requests received	35	52	56	39	30	35	41
Accepted	15	37	46	35	30	30	40
Under consideration	7	7	7	3	2	4	1
Supplementary requests	10	24	50	26	33	41	40
Number of Countries making requests	16	22	23	27	30	31	23
Section 2 Notices issued for MLA	109	141	262	181	261	206	274
Search Warrants executed for MLA	0	0	0	2	10	8	0

From January 2006, under the Proceeds of Crime Act 2002, the SFO has been able to assist countries in matters of restraint and confiscation. Currently, the Restraint Unit is assisting both India and Switzerland with their requests.

MLA statistics for 2005-06 record the highest level of incoming letters of request for the last four years. Section 2 Notices served for the purpose of obtaining evidence on behalf of requesting states is the highest since the MLA unit was created in 1995.

Frauds perpetrated throughout the world are becoming more complex and multi-national. Criminals are crossing international boundaries in an attempt to perpetrate fraud and hide the proceeds of crime. It is therefore no surprise to see that the level of assistance requested from overseas authorities this year has been more extensive, requiring greater in depth participation by members of the MLA Unit. Apart from using our domestic powers to obtain evidence on behalf of overseas authorities, the MLA Unit also offers advice and direction to Prosecutors when there is a need to seek evidence in other jurisdictions.

Apart from operational assistance, the MLA Unit has also provided a number of formal presentations to representatives from countries including, Slovakia, The Netherlands, China, Japan, India, Zimbabwe, Kenya, Taiwan, Jamaica, Czech Republic, France, Georgia and Serbia.

During the year, the MLA Unit has continued to work closely with other law enforcement agencies in the U.K. including HM Revenue & Customs, the CPS and the FSA. Both NCIS and the Metropolitan Police continue to offer support when requested. Liaison with lawyers and senior Police officers from these agencies is encouraged and annual MLA meetings at the Home Office foster greater collaboration on an inter-agency level. Such co-operation reflects the increasing desire among law enforcement agencies to respond to overseas requests in a professional and organised manner which will enhance the reputation of the U.K. in the area of international mutual legal assistance.

Management and Operations

The SFO has a multi-disciplinary approach to the investigation and prosecution of serious and complex fraud. Each case is allocated to a team that includes lawyers, investigators, information technology and other specialists, law clerks and police officers. The SFO makes extensive use of private sector expertise as necessary, for example employing private sector accountants to assist in investigations and using counsel to prosecute.

Each operating division is made up of lawyers, accountants and other specialist financial investigators and support staff. Inter-disciplinary teams, each headed by a case controller, are formed from within operating divisions to deal with cases allotted to them, and case budgets are delegated. Management information systems provide the Director with information on case budgets, expenditure, timetables and he meets with each division monthly to discuss the cases and their progress.

The SFO operates a delegated budgeting system to encourage value for money, and budgeting rounds are held two or three times a year. Case budgets are delegated to case controllers and are reviewed as necessary in the light of changes in case plans and the SFO undertakes monthly reviews of expenditure throughout the financial year to ensure that expenditure stays within provision. Working procedures and management information needs are part of the strategic reviews that are continuing.

Systems for risk management are in place and regular reviews take place at the relevant levels within the organisation. The Strategic and Operational Boards regularly monitor the identified key risks to the organisation. They are aided in this by the work of the Audit Committee which promotes and provides support on key overall corporate governance issues to the Director. Development of financial and information systems continues and these will improve the management and delivery of the SFO aim and objectives. Improvements are planned to provide capture and dissemination of more timely and accurate information to managers within the SFO to support decision making, the achievement of objectives and accountability.

The SFO seeks to achieve a cost-effective balance between permanent and temporary staff and keeps its staffing plans under review so that staff numbers can be accommodated within administration costs provision. At 31 March 2006, the SFO had 10 members of the Senior Civil Service, falling within the salary bands indicated in the second table below.

Staff Numbers

Staff years	1999-00 Actual	2000-01 Actual	2001-02 Actual	2002-03 Actual	2003-04 Actual	2004-05 Actual	2005-06 Actual	2006-07 Plans	2007-08 Plans
Civil service full Time equivalents	166	169	210	232	238	247	290	300	300
Overtime	2	1	3	2	2	2	2	2	2
Casuals	9	22	3	18	14	12	10	10	10
Total	**177**	**192**	**216**	**252**	**254**	**261**	**302**	**312**	**312**

Senior Civil Service Salaries

£5,000 Bands	Number of staff
£65,000 – 69,999	1
£70,000 – 74,999	3
£75,000 – 79,999	2
£85,000 – 89,999	1
£90,000 – 94,999	1
£100,000 – 104,999	1
£155,000 – 159,999	1

Use of Information Technology

The Computer Forensic Unit (CFU) of the Serious Fraud Office is responsible for the acquisition and investigation of case relevant data from seized electronic devices. Nearly all SFO cases involve the analysis of computer data and the CFU contributes expertise and equipment to aid case investigators with this task. Keeping pace with change and especially volumes is a constant challenge. The CFU continually strives to meet these challenges and is heavily involved in the research and development of new techniques. The development of a mobile forensic laboratory capability to enable computer-based material to be accessed at the scene of a search rather than having to remove the hardware to a remote laboratory will improve the delivery and the effectiveness of the CFU team.

The DOCMAN system supports the Office's case work from the initial acquisition and creation of documents through to the presentation of the case in Court. It involves scanning all the case documents in to a computer system so that case workers work on computerised images rather than paper documents and will provide enhanced capability to produce documentation sets needed for prosecution purposes. It provides provenance and continuity of evidence materials. Decisions on acceptance and implementation of the DOCMAN system were taken in 2004-05, following the production of the full business case, to support the key targets of reductions in the length of case investigation and prosecution time. Development of the system has continued during the year and more is planned for the future, based on regular reviews and assessment of performance and project stage completion. The focus of activity is now on taking the existing functions and making then easier to use, thus freeing investigators from the minutiae of using systems and allowing them more time for analysis and other value-added activity. At 31 March 2006, 31 cases were using the system.

The dependence of the SFO on information systems to carry out its daily operations continues to increase, particularly in relation to handling documentation, investigation and collaborative working. During the year work has continued on:

- The replacement cycle at the level of desktop machines is now complete and a planned turnover of stock is in place. The office is well placed to further support off-site working and improve information presentation;
- Continuous review of the information technology strategy to ensure best value and placement to be able to respond to continuing IT changes;
- Rationalising the different types and versions of software used for investigation work is now complete. Planned organisation wide lifts of software are now in planning. A software applications and licensing audit is underway;
- Continuous review of security in accordance with government policy and the migration from ISO 17799 to the successor ISO27001;
- Further revision and testing of Business Continuity Plans to reflect changes and improved response capability;
- Upgrades to finance system to provide further basis for improved management information and support decision making;
- Advancing plans for HR records management and realigning of the recruitment strategy and processes;
- Plans for electronic records management (ERM) and archiving to comply with central requirements and support access under the Data Protection Act and Freedom of Information (FOI) requests;
- Extending collaborative work for the use of technology support and standards for electronic presentation of evidence in courts and proceedings;
- Implementing and reviewing strategy for an office-wide intranet and knowledge management initiatives.

Departmental Investment Strategy

The capital provision published in the SR 2004 settlement details the total available to the department for administrative capital. All current and capital expenditure supports core operational functionality and is planned, as far as possible, to take account of changing circumstances which may affect these operations, in advance of their occurrence. The SFO continues to seek value for money on all procurement and contracts. Given the small size of the SFO, this is most effectively carried out through maximising use of framework contracts set up by the Office of Government Commerce and continuing partnerships with other public sector organisations that have dedicated resources working in these areas. The SFO is also looking at ways of leveraging better value through sharing of common services with sister organisations.

The SFO has not historically been asset rich. Headquarters office space is occupied on a full repairing lease and a programme of current maintenance expenditure to support and improve the fabric of the property has been agreed. With the planned increase in SFO permanent staff, Elm House has become incapable of supporting the SFO's total space needs. The SFO has leased additional office space close to Elm House and has advanced its plans for meeting longer term accommodation maintenance responsibilities. The additional capital provision available from 2004-05 was a step change and provided the opportunity for the office to reconsider its investment plans and to seek to provide the tools to further promote effectiveness and efficiency. As a component of this the capital employed by the SFO and plans for the future have an increasing impact on our ability to deliver the aims and objectives of the office (see table below).

SFO Capital Employed

	1999-00 Outturn	2000-01 Outturn	2001-02 Outturn	2002-03 Outturn	2003-04 Outturn	2004-05 Outturn	2005-06 Provisional Outturn	2006-07 Plan	2007-08 Plan
Assets on balance sheet at end of year: Fixed assets: Tangible *of which:* Other Equipment	39	42	42	54	67	140	130	200	300
Computer equipment	97	220	298	334	1,160	1,987	2,620	3,300	3,300
Intangible					**168**	**168**			
	136	**262**	**340**	**378**	**1,395**	**2,284**	**2,750**	**3,500**	**3,500**
Current assets	3,496	1,168	780	4,621	2,627	2,740	2,000	2,000	2,000
Creditors (<1 year)	3,074	1,840	2,676	6,292	4,049	5,890	3,000	3,000	3,000
Provisions	348	307	353	379	289	209	300	300	300
Capital employed	**210**	**–717**	**–1,909**	**–1,662**	**–316**	**–883**	**2,050**	**2,800**	**2,800**

Resource Budget

Expenditure on administration includes current costs and the costs of capital spending. Administration expenditure includes general costs associated with the running of the office and covers such items as staff costs, other general administrative expenditure, IT services and accommodation costs. Investigation and prosecution programme expenditure covers Counsel fees, witness expenses and other direct case investigation and prosecution costs. No specific provision to cover very large cases has been made in plans. Both the incidence and size of such cases is unpredictable and the subject of individual negotiation with the Treasury. Details of the resource budget outturn and future plans are given in the table below.

Resource Budget for the Serious Fraud Office — **£000**

	2000-01 Outturn	2001-02 Outturn	2002-03 Outturn	2003-04 Outturn	2004-05 Outturn	2005-06 Estimated Outturn	2006-07 Plans	2007-08 Plans
Serious Fraud Office	19,636	23,030	26,214	27,791	32,808	40,351	35,802	35,802
Of which:								
Serious Fraud Office	19,636	23,030	26,214	27,791	32,808	40,351	35,802	35,802
Total Resource Budget	19,636	23,030	26,214	27,791	32,808	40,351	35,802	35,802

Counsel Fees and Costs Awarded Against the SFO

Spending on counsel fees, a major component of programme expenditure and costs awarded against the SFO is given in the table below:

Counsel fees and costs awarded against the SFO — **£000s**

	Outturn 1999-00	Outturn 2000-01	Outturn 2001-02	Outturn 2002-03	Outturn 2003-04	Outturn 2004-05	Provisional Outturn 2005-06
Counsel fees	2,461	3,320	4,322	4,000	4,306	3,748	3,900
Costs awarded	0	0	0	0	18	98	822

Environmental Matters

Along with other Law Officer's departments the SFO is working towards the targets set for sustainable development on the Government Estate. We continue to monitor energy consumption and strive to ensure that prudent use is made of these resources. The DOCMAN project and office IT strategy maintain our progression and commitment towards using less paper in the office and in the presentation of our cases for trial. Sustainable resource considerations form a key component of the current upgrade works at our Elm House Headquarters. Environmental considerations form a part of our general procurement process.

Staffing

As at 31 March 2006, the SFO had 290 permanent staff compared with 272 at 31 March 2005. These figures exclude fixed-term employees, consultants, counsel employed on individual cases and police officers working within the Office.

Recruitment has been ongoing throughout the year, particularly in relation to investigative and support staff. There have been a number of occasions where permitted exceptions to fair and open competition have been used. The resource needs of SFO cases are such that it proves necessary, from time to time, to appoint staff on short term contracts, particularly to provide support to off-site case teams.

The SFO is committed to treating all applicants fairly and reasonably irrespective of their ethnic or national origin, sex, marital status, sexual orientation, religion or disability. Our processes are kept under regular review to ensure that any indicators of bias are highlighted and tackled. The SFO is similarly committed to treat all its employees fairly. The table below analyses staff by grade and shows the number of women, ethnic minority and disabled staff in post at 31 March 2006. During the year the SFO has reissued its policy documents on Equality and Diversity, and Dignity at Work.

Permanent women, ethnic minority and disabled staff

Band	No. of posts	Women	Ethnic Minority	Disabled People
SCS	10	3	0	1
G7 – G6	78	31	10	1
HEO – SEO	75	22	11	3
EO	79	45	27	3
AO	48	28	17	1
Total	**290**	**129**	**65**	**9**

Human Resource Management

This year we have continued our work to improve the way staff are managed, assessed and rewarded. We have:

- Started to review the appraisal process for staff below the Senior Civil Service, in order to promote a more consistent approach to performance assessment, objective setting and identifying development needs;
- Operated a Special Bonus Committee, formed from a cross section of staff, which meets to consider nominations for special awards for work of particular merit; and
- Continued our major reviews of recruitment and training strategies to ensure that skills and the availability of those skills better match business needs. Recruitment processes have also been improved through the introdution of electronic application forms.

Training and development remains a major priority for the SFO. We encourage development amongst our staff, including those who demonstrate the commitment and ability to obtain external qualifications. The Office is an accredited Investor in People and is approved to train solicitors and take pupil barristers. We also have Approved Employer status for the Association of Chartered and Certified Accountants.

Sickness Absences

Sick absence for 2005 resulted in an average of 6.75 days per employee.

2004 Spending Review

The 2004 Spending Review was conducted fully in resource terms. It set plans for public spending for 2005-06 to 2007-08. No additional resources were provided in the SR2004 settlement and it did not take account of any inflationary pressures. The SFO's SR2004 settlement incorporated Efficiency Review targets to make non-cashable efficiency savings of £3.5 million within the settlement time-frame and applicable to three of the efficiency workstreams. The SFO has committed to deliver these, has put the necessary governance structures in place and will regularly review and publish progress against plans.

Delivery of the 2005-06 targets is progressing well and there appears to be low risk to future delivery. At the December 2005 report stage savings achieved totalled £2 million (non-cashable) and were ahead of plans in total mainly due to the accommodation strategy change. Activity in the corporate services workstream delivered improved management information, reduced recruitment cycle times, better focused recruitment advertisement and rationalised the employment of temporary staff. The procurement stream resulted in the accommodation strategy change to a cost effective alternative (noted above), reduced costs of scanning and some rationalisation of IT infrastructure and service costs. In the productivity stream the DOCMAN system contributed to more effective case management and progress. In addition to continuing savings from accommodation, which should yield £1.3 million, gains from the other streams are planned to yield £0.7 million over the next year (December 2005–December 2006). Work on measurement and quality control continues and details of plans for efficiency delivery by workstream are published on the SFO website. The table below illustrates the main components.

Efficiency Review Targets				
Efficiency Review Timeframe:				**TOTALS**
Year	**2005-06**	**2006-07**	**2007-08**	
Target efficiencies:	**£m**	**£m**	**£m**	**£m**
SR2004 Settlement	**1.13**	**2.0**	**2.815**	**5.945**
Efficiency By Workstream:				
Productive Time				
DOCMAN	0.3	0.6	1	1.9
Scanning	0.2	0.2	0.2	0.6
Electronic Presentation of Evidence	0.02	0.02	0.06	0.1
TOTAL	**0.52**	**0.82**	**1.26**	**2.6**
Procurement				
Consultants	0.05	0.05	0.15	0.25
FM	0.01	0.01	0.01	0.03
Accommodation	1.4	1.6	2.0	5.0
TOTAL	**1.46**	**1.66**	**2.16**	**5.28**
Corporate Services				
Recruitment	0.01	0.01	0.01	0.03
Temp Staff	0.04	0.04	0.04	0.12
TOTAL	**0.05**	**0.05**	**0.05**	**0.15**
Total Baseline Savings:	**2.03**	**2.53**	**3.47**	**8.03**

2005-06 Outturn

The provisional outturn for 2005-06 is £40.4 million.

Public Spending Plans and Regional Expenditure:

Public spending plans are shown in the table below. All SFO expenditure, by its nature, cannot be analysed by the country or region of the UK for whose benefit it has been expended except to say that expenditure is incurred mainly in London and the South East where SFO headquarters is based.

Total public spending for the SFO								£000
	2000-01 Outturn	2001-02 Outturn	2002-03 Outturn	2003-04 Outturn	2004-05 Outturn	2005-06 Estimated Outturn	2006-07 Plans	2007-08 Plans
Consumption of resources:								
Reducing fraud and the risk of fraud, and delivering justice and the rule of law	19,636	23,030	26,214	27,791	32,808	40,351	35,802	35,802
Total resource budget	**19,636**	**23,030**	**26,214**	**27,791**	**32,808**	**40,351**	**35,802**	**35,802**
of which:								
Resource DEL	19,636	23,030	26,214	27,791	32,808	40,351	35,802	35,802
Capital spending:								
Reducing fraud and the risk of fraud, and delivering justice and the rule of law	241	256	228	1,052	2,060	2,750	3,500	3,500
Total capital budget	**241**	**256**	**228**	**1,052**	**2,060**	**2,750**	**3,500**	**3,500**
of which:								
Capital DEL	241	256	228	1,052	2,060	2,750	3,500	3,500
Total public spending[1]	**19,762**	**23,108**	**26,259**	**28,234**	**33,772**	**41,001**	**37,702**	**37,702**

[1] Total public spending calculated as the total of the resource budget plus the capital budget, less depreciation.

Further Information

Further information on the work of the SFO may be obtained from:

Serious Fraud Office
Elm House
10-16 Elm Street
London WC1X 0BJ

Telephone number: 020 7239 7272
Fax number: 020 7837 1689
Website: www.sfo.gov.uk

4

Treasury Solicitor's Department

TSol (Treasury Solicitor's Department Agency)
Attorney General's Office
HM Crown Prosecution Service Inspectorate
Treasury Solicitor's Department Tables

TREASURY SOLICITOR'S DEPARTMENT

Introduction

The HM Procurator General and Treasury Solicitor's Department Estimate covers:

- TSol, which includes the Treasury Solicitor's Department Agency and the Government Legal Service Secretariat (GLS Secretariat);
- The Attorney General's Office (AGO) previously the Legal Secretariat to the Law Officers (pages 91-94); and
- HM Crown Prosecution Service Inspectorate (HMCPSI) (pages 95-101).

TSol provides legal services to Departments of central government and to other publicly funded bodies, and collects bona vacantia on behalf of the Crown. TSol's two main work streams are Litigation and Advisory legal services.

The GLS Secretariat supports the Treasury Solicitor in her role as Head of the Government Legal Service. It develops policies that enhance the reputation, effectiveness and corporate cohesiveness of the GLS.

Receipts from client departments meet over 90 per cent of the costs of the work undertaken by TSol (either through hourly fees or a per capitation charge rate). This part of the Estimate operates on net administration costs control. The public interest work undertaken by TSol and the other areas of the Estimate are met by funds voted by Parliament.

TSol was established as an Executive Agency in April 1996 and moved to net administration costs control in April 1999. The Agency is led by HM Procurator General and Treasury Solicitor (currently Dame Juliet Wheldon DCB QC), in the role of Agency Chief Executive. Ministerial oversight of all the areas covered by the Estimate rests with the Attorney General.

Organisation and Management Structure

The Treasury Solicitor, as Chief Executive and Accounting Officer of TSol is supported in delivering her responsibilities by the Executive and Supervisory Boards.

The Executive Board is a small group of directors representing different Agency business areas – litigation, advisory work, and corporate services – attended monthly by the three non executive directors. It is the main decision making body and supports the Chief Executive in delivering the Agency's objectives.

The Supervisory Board (SB) includes all TSol directors plus the non-executive directors. The role of SB is to advise the Chief Executive on the broad strategic direction of TSol business and provide collective leadership across the department. It also acts as a key stakeholder group for assessing the impact of improvement activity on the business.

Internal Control

TSol's senior management have implemented a programme of improvements in internal control and management systems. These include:

- Establishing 3 programme boards, one for each key focus area – Client Care, Business Systems and Human Resources;
- Using TSol's Business Strategy Unit to co-ordinate and support senior management in risk management, business planning, programme management and performance measurement;
- Improved risk registers for individual Divisions and ensuring there is consistency between Divisional and TSol risk registers; and
- A review of our client base, that resulted in the production of guidance for dealing with clients' legal risks.

TSol has an Audit Committee which supports the Accounting Officer by monitoring and reviewing the department's risk, control and governance processes, and the associated assurance processes. The committee, which meets three times a year, is chaired by an independent member and includes three Non Executive Directors.

A Security Committee in TSol oversees security policy and practice, including IT security and Physical Audits. TSol is compliant with the BS7799 standard for information security management.

Management Structure

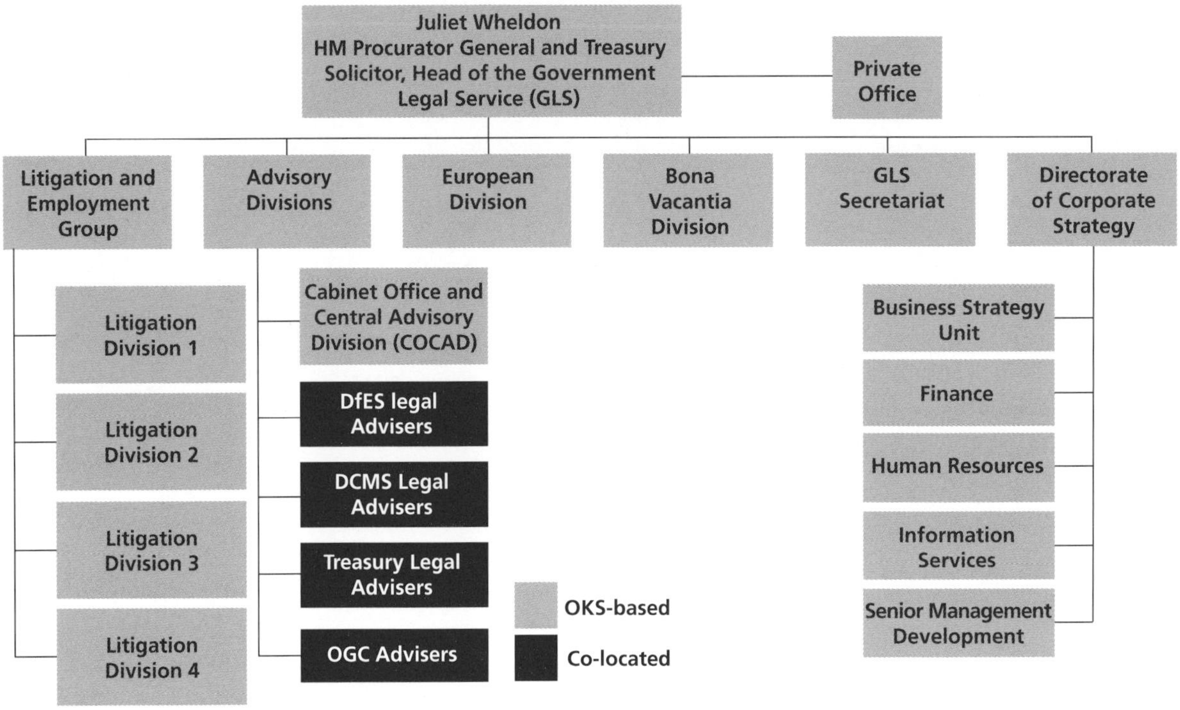

TSol Performance and Resources

Aim and Objective

Aim: *to be our clients' best choice for the services we provide.*

Objective: *to provide high quality, value for money, legal services that meet the needs of our clients; to collect bona vacantia on behalf of the Crown; to give our staff the opportunity to develop themselves and their careers; and thus maintain a high reputation for TSol as a whole.*

TSol have published a Corporate Plan to cover the years 2005-2008. One target TSol have set themselves is to be consistently seen by their clients as being their best choice.

To achieve this TSol are focussed on three key strategic areas:

- Satisfied clients;
- Satisfied staff; and
- Best practice systems.

Targets

Our business targets for 2005-06 were as set out in the Corporate Plan (2005-08):

for Client Service:

- To meet client satisfaction ratings measured by % of clients rating TSol services as 'Good' or 'Excellent'
  - At least 95% for Advisory Divisions
  - At least 95% for Litigation Division and ECCG

for Cost:

- To recover from clients the full operating costs for chargeable services
- To maintain corporate service staff costs at no more than 14% of total staff costs

for Government Productivity and Efficiency Targets:

- To pay all undisputed supplier invoices in accordance with terms or within 30 days

Performance Against Targets 2005-06

Performance Measures	Latest Outturn	
Client Satisfaction		
Client satisfaction ratings as measured by % of clients rating TSol 'Good' or 'Excellent'	Target: Latest Outturn Advisory: Latest Outturn Litigation:	95% 97% 97%
Cost		
Maintain corporate staff overhead costs at no more than 14% of total staff costs	Target: Latest Outturn:	14% 13% (Pd 9)
Recover full operating costs of chargeable services		Met
Government Productivity & Efficiency Targets		
Pay all undisputed supplier invoices in accordance with terms or within 30 days	Latest Outturn:	96%

Efficiency Programme

The targets for the efficiency savings and the work force reductions to be achieved by March 2008 which were set in the 2004 Spending Review are:

Non-cashable savings	Cashable Savings	Headcount reduction
£1.2m	£1.8m	36

The baselines for cost savings and for the workforce reductions are 2003-04. To meet this target savings of £0.3m (£0.1m non-cashable and £0.2m cashable) were planned, and achieved, for 2005-06 and action is in hand to deliver an additional £0.3m required in 2006-07 to remain on target. The target for workforce reductions as a result of these savings is 36 posts by the end of 2007-08 and 10 have already been delivered.

Over the next year TSol will focus on achieving the twin goals of genuine efficiency and providing better quality services at lower cost to the client. TSol will therefore be looking to reduce the costs of the business by improving business processes, information systems and infrastructure. TSol will also be looking closely at the organisation and delivery of core work to ensure it is delivered cost effectively. This, added to the central initiatives for procurement and shared services, will help TSol to deliver the final year of Spending Review 2004 savings, and to ensure best value for its clients.

The Agency's work

TSol is structured to meet the needs of its clients. The work of each Division is summarised below.

Litigation Group provides civil litigation services to the majority of Government Departments and many other publicly funded bodies. It is one of the largest civil litigation practices in the country. Some 11,000 Litigation and Employment cases are opened and handled each year. The Group recovers the majority of its costs by billing client Departments for its time.

Employment and Commercial Contracts Group was consolidated into the Litigation and Employment Group in February 2006. It is one of the largest employment practices in the country. It provides employment litigation and advisory services to Government Departments and other publicly funded bodies. The costs of the Group are met by clients, through a mix of capitation and hourly fee charging.

Advisory Divisions provide legal advice to Ministers and officials of the Departments for Culture, Media and Sport; Department for Education and Skills; the Office of Government Commerce; and HM Treasury. Each of these Divisions is co-located with their principal client. The Cabinet Office and Central Advisory Division (COCAD), based at the Agency's headquarters, provides legal advice to the Cabinet Office and to a number of smaller Departments and publicly funded bodies (as do certain of the other advisory divisions). The full cost of advisory work is recovered from clients, through a mix of per capitation and hourly fee charging.

European Division provides and co-ordinates legal services in support of the Government's policies in relation to the European Union. It advises the European Secretariat of the Cabinet Office, conducts all litigation on behalf of the UK in the European Court of Justice, and through co-ordination seeks to ensure a consistent approach to questions of Community law across UK Government Departments and the Northern Ireland, Scottish and Welsh administrations. The cost of the Division's work has hitherto been funded by the Estimate. Alternative methods of funding are being explored and a levy on client departments will be introduced to meet part of the costs of the European Litigation team in 2006-07.

Bona Vacantia Division acts on behalf of the Crown to collect and dispose of ownerless assets arising from the estates of people who die intestate and without relatives entitled to inherit, and from dissolved companies in England and Wales (except for the Duchies of Cornwall and Lancaster). The Division handled more than 10,000 new cases in 2005-6. The costs of the Division are met from receipts.

Government Legal Service Secretariat (the Secretariat) is a separate unit within TSol whose purpose is to provide effective advice and support to the GLS and to the Treasury Solicitor as Head of the GLS in support of her role in providing leadership and strategic direction to the Service.

Directorate of Corporate Strategy (DOCS) has responsibility for planning and implementing strategic, business and policy development throughout TSol. The cost of DOCS is apportioned over the operational areas of the Department and recovered, as appropriate, through charges to clients and from the Estimate.

People

As at 1 April 2005 there were 722 staff in post in TSol and AGO of which 40% were male and 60% were female. 155 staff were recorded as non-respondents or non-participants in the disability and ethnic origin surveys.

Of those who participated in those surveys, 4% declared a disability and 18.6% were from ethnic minorities.

There were 37 promotions in the period 1 April 2005 to 31 December 2005. Of those promoted 2 had declared a disability; 59% were male and 41% female. Of those promoted who declared their origin were 81% white and 19% ethnic minorities.

These figures do not include HMCPSI, who run their own equal opportunities policy and race equality scheme under the Race Relations Amendment Act 2000.

Paybill and Senior Civil Service (SCS)

More than 71% of the total gross administration costs for the Department are pay related. The paybill figure includes salaries paid to members of the SCS. On 1 April 2005 the SCS salaries were:

Salary Band £k	No. of Staff
55 – 59,999	6
60 – 64,999	3
65 – 69,999	12
70 – 74,999	9
75 – 79,999	15
80 – 84,999	5
85 – 89,999	2
90 – 94,999	5
95 – 99,999	3
100 – 104,999	1
105 – 109,999	1
110 – 114,999	2
115 – 124,999	2
125 – 134,999	0
135 – 144,999	0
145 – 149,999	0
150 – 154,999	0
155 – 159,999	1
TOTAL	**67**

Recruitment Information

The Department is bound by the Civil Service Commissioners rules on fair and open competition and selection on merit. Systems are subject to internal review and TSol and AGO were last audited on behalf of the Commissioners in 2005. TSol completed an on-line self-assessment on compliance with the OCSC Recruitment code in 2005. The feedback was that TSol was compliant.

Between 1 April 2005 and 31 December 2005, 40 new members of staff were recruited to the Department by means of fair and open competition.

Grade	Number	Male	Female	Ethnic Minority	Disabled
Grade 7	18	7	11	2	
Legal Officer	11	4	7	1	
Legal Trainee	8	2	6	0	
Administrative Grades (SEO, HEO, EO, AO, PS and SGB)	4	4	0	0	
TOTAL	**41**	**17**	**24**	**3**	**7%**

During the period specified above, exceptions to the OCSC Recruitment Code were used on eight occasions. Of these, four were extensions to casual contracts where projects or work on Public Inquiries had extended beyond the expected end date. These figures do not include HMCPSI, who run their own recruitment policies and practice.

Value for Money

As the provider of civil litigation services across government, a key TSol aim is to provide value for money to its clients. TSol has a specific target to minimise overhead costs. The Agency has taken a number of initiatives, such as building on the L-CAT partnership with OGC, in order to help client departments achieve value for money when purchasing legal services from the private sector.

The use of consultants within the Agency has been reviewed, and recommendations from the review are being implemented, to ensure that temporary staff perform well and provide value for money.

Modernising TSol

The Attorney General's Vision

TSol supports the Attorney General's vision through strengthening TSol's capability to deliver, building strong relationships across government, particularly with its clients, and by taking positive steps to strengthen its position as an employer of choice.

The focus for modernising TSol has been:

- Strengthening the capability to deliver
  - Improving governance
  - Improving Information Systems
  - Improving accommodation
  - Developing a consistent Corporate Identity
- Building strong partnerships with clients
- Becoming an employer of choice

Capability to Deliver

Governance

At the end of 04-05 TSol decided to review its governance structures to simplify and rationalise existing networks of committees, and clarify roles and responsibilities.

The role of the Executive Board has been clarified and strengthened and a new corporate approach to risk identification and management has been introduced across executive board, programme boards and DOCS. The Executive Board has also been strengthened by the appointment of a third non-executive director with a particular focus on business and IT.

In May 2005 three new programme boards were introduced to oversee key elements of the work programme, linked to TSol's main objectives – satisfied clients, satisfied staff and best practice systems. The terms of reference, membership, work programmes and risk registers were signed off and are reviewed by the Executive Board quarterly.

The Departmental Audit Committee has acknowledged the review and outcomes as a significant improvement.

Information Systems Strategy

TSol IS Strategy was agreed in October 2005. The strategy focuses on procuring off the shelf packages reflecting Cabinet Office best practice. The focus in the first phase is to deliver better billing information for clients, improved time recording, better management information and greater pro-activity on FOI in respect of Bona Vacantia. Work is also underway on procuring an HR database system in joint co-operation with CPS.

Electronic Document and Records Management (eRIK)

A project to deliver electronic records management to the non-litigation part of the business was successfully piloted and went live in European and COCAD Divisions in January 2005. It will be rolled out to all other areas within scope by May 2006. This will contribute to the Modernising Government requirement that all documents created electronically can be stored and managed electronically.

Legal Information Online Network (LION)

LION was originally launched in January 2002 in response to the growing need for an inter-departmental intranet to promote joined-up working and sharing valuable information and experience for lawyers across Government. LION was redesigned and relaunched in conjunction with the Knowledge Network in October 2005.

Move to One Kemble Street and a New Corporate Identity

Much of TSol moved to new open plan accommodation at One Kemble Street in September 2005. The accommodation provides a modern, flexible business environment benefiting both clients and staff. Planning the move was a major project, which has been completed on time and within budget. Proceeds from the sale of the Queen Anne's Chambers premises exceeded the £30m asking price. All proceeds have been passed to HM Treasury as a Consolidated Fund Excess Receipt.

Work continues on measuring and evaluating the key benefits set out in the project's October 2003 Business Case:

- Improving the quality of the working environment,
- Removing the block to cultural change represented by Queen Anne's Chambers, and
- Providing the capacity to deal with further business growth.

The new corporate identity, shown to staff in October 2004 was implemented in May 2005. The "TSol" identity reflects our development as a modern, professional legal practice following the Quinquennial review in 2001.

Sustainable Development

The Department's business provides limited opportunity to subscribe directly to wider environmental policy formulation and to the Sustainable Development in Government initiative. The Solicitor General is the responsible Green Minister and TSol, together with the other Law Officer's Departments, reports to him on all relevant issues.

The Department has a Green Housekeeping Policy and a Green Transport Plan, which are kept under review and which all staff are encouraged to follow (e.g. energy efficiency, recycling paper, etc). The department also recycles fluorescent tubes and toner cartridges and seeks to purchase environmentally friendly goods (e.g. recycled paper, cleaning consumables) and services (e.g. the GCDA Green Taxi service) wherever possible.

The Department will, with other Law Officers' Departments, be playing its part in meeting the targets set for the Government Estate and an Action Plan for 2006 is currently in the process of being agreed between the Law Officers' Departments.

Freedom of Information

TSol has developed a process for dealing with requests under the FoI Act to ensure that the Agency is compliant with its obligations under the Act. A Supervisory Board member oversees each request and the Departmental Records Officer (DRO) co-ordinates responses. The DRO is supported by Information Liaison Officers who have been appointed to represent their team across TSol.

Regulatory Reform Action Plan

TSol is not a regulatory department and has no actions to be completed in the Action Plan.

Building Strong Partnerships

Client Care

High quality, added value client care is a priority for TSol and achieving the objective of satisfied clients is vital to maintaining its high reputation. In 2005 the Client Care Programme Board was created to focus on client issues, deliver an agreed client care work programme for 05-06 and manage the strategic risk of potential damage to TSol's reputation.

TSol has:

- revised the client brochure to reflect TSol's new standards and the opportunities for clients as a result of the move to One Kemble Street;
- issued annual reports to three major clients – IND, Home Office and Prison Service;
- provided fourteen newsletters for a number of clients covering a range of issues from employment cases to public inquiries;
- appointed client care managers for 49 major clients;
- created a network group for client care managers to share best practice and support the Client Care Programme Board in delivering improved client care.

Work continues on:

- redeveloping the client care intranet site, giving client care managers and all TSol staff access to information such as TSol's client care principles and standards, managing clients, Lexcel compliant processes for handling complaints and information on client feedback and how to obtain it;
- reviewing the approach to supplying training to clients to identify further opportunities to add value;
- evaluating TSol's approach to supporting and developing client care managers and other client-facing staff.

Client Feedback

TSol consistently achieves high ratings in its client satisfaction surveys. In 2005 the Litigation and Employment Groups improved their performance and achieved a 97.8% satisfaction rate of good or excellent compared to the target of 95%. The Advisory Legal Teams also exceeded the target, achieving 97.6% satisfaction rate of good or excellent.

Litigation and ECCG

The graph below shows the percentage of clients rating TSol 'Good' or 'Excellent' in relation to the performance of Litigation and ECCG staff. These results were gathered in 2005, using the client satisfaction survey methodology established in 2004.

% of Litigation/ ECCG clients rating TSol as 'Good' or 'Excellent'

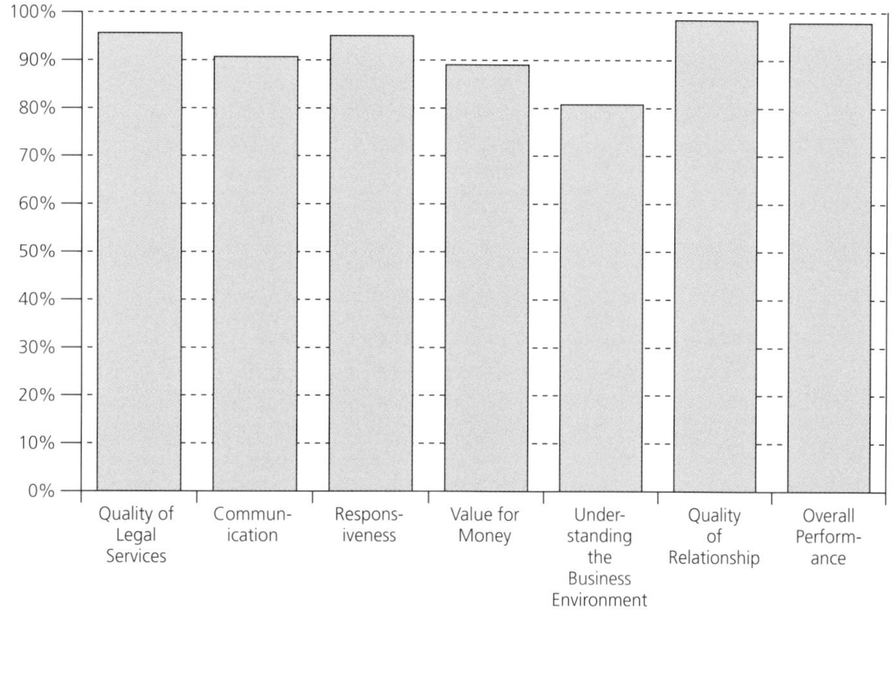

Advisory

The 2005 Advisory client satisfaction survey achieved a 97.6% satisfaction rate of 'Good' or 'Excellent' compared to the target of 95%. The graph below shows the percentage of clients rating TSol as 'Good' and 'Excellent' in relation to the performance of Advisory Division staff. These results were gathered in February 2006 using methodology established in 2003.

% of Advisory clients rating TSol as 'Good' or 'Excellent'

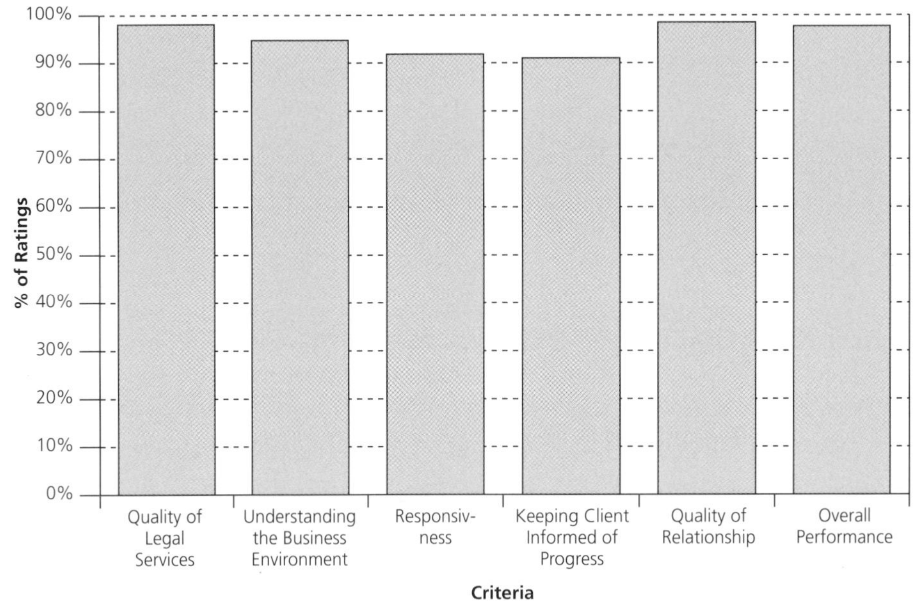

Becoming an Employer of Choice

TSol is fully supportive of the Attorney General's vision in becoming an employer of choice. TSol relies on and values its staff and wants them to contribute fully and have the opportunity to develop. The Agency is proud to be recognised as meeting the Investors in People standard, and to hold the two tick Disability Symbol.

TSol is committed to ensuring all its staff have the opportunity to acquire the competencies necessary to perform effectively in their current role and to meet the challenges of changing business needs. Managers have a key role to play and TSol support includes training, guidance and advice. Support for senior managers include HR Account Managers – senior members of HR who offer advice on day-to-day management issues. TSol is also implementing the Civil Service 10 Point Diversity Plan championed by the Head of the Civil Service.

Human Resources activities are co-ordinated through the HR Programme Board. The work has included:

- Incorporating Professional Skills for Government (PSG) core skills into key HR policies.
- Improving leadership in TSol.
- Preparing TSol for IIP re-accreditation.
- Reviewing performance management and reward strategies.

TSol uses a programme of staff surveys, Investors in People (IIP) Reviews, team meetings, open forums and Directors Question Time (an intranet noticeboard) to listen and respond to the views of its staff. It is seeking reaffirmation of its IIP status in 2006. The revised IIP Standard places emphasis on leadership and will provide valuable information on where progress has been made to address issues and on what more needs to be done.

In 2005, TSol introduced a child-care voucher scheme and in 2006 staff will be able to take advantage of a health screening service.

TSol enjoys a good working relationship with trade unions. This was enhanced in March 2005 by TSol and the Trade Union Side signing a Partnership Agreement.

In September 2005, TSol launched a streamlined, objective driven appraisal process which takes account of the Professional Skills for Government (PSG) Framework. Work was taken forward, liaising with the wider Government Legal Service (GLS) on embedding PSG requirements in TSol's job descriptions, development provision and selection processes. The PSG skills audit undertaken in Autumn 2005 will help determine TSol's learning and development programme for 2006. A second audit conducted towards the end of 2006 will assess progress.

As part of the 2005 GLS Planning and Development Review, TSol conducted a systematic review of its legal staff. TSol continues to use secondments to broaden individual experience. Schemes such as Judicial Assistants, European Commission Structural Traineeships and Preparing for Top Management are used to bring on talent.

The continuous recruitment campaign for Government lawyers has enabled TSol to recruit high quality lawyers to meet its business needs. TSol continues to use a limited proportion of temporary staff in both legal and administrative areas to manage volatility in the demand for its services. TSol's administrative staff continue to provide an important support service. TSol recognises opportunities for administrative career progression within TSol are limited compared with what it can offer lawyers. TSol continues to focus on enabling its administrative staff to develop transferable skills and encouraging movement between teams to gain broader experience.

Health & Safety

A Health and Safety Committee continues to work to ensure that Health and Safety issues within the Department are handled within the principles of corporate governance as laid down by the revitalising Health and Safety initiative. The Committee's duties include keeping Health and Safety policy and practice under review; considering suggestions put forward by Committee members and staff more generally as to improvements in the Department's Health and Safety regime; and promoting awareness of Health and Safety issues in order to encourage staff to achieve high safety standards.

TSol is committed to maintaining levels of Health and Safety within One Kemble Street.

2006-07 Resource Estimate

The overall Net Resource Requirement for 2006-07 is £13.2m: £1.0 m less than 2005-06. This is partly due to a £0.6m reduction in TSol's net administration costs for 2006-07. This reflects the transfer of provision to Departments which use the services of TSol's European Division, following a decision to introduce a levy based charging system, based on usage. The AGO's provision in 2006-07 is £0.5 m lower than in 2005-06. In 2005-06 there was a reallocation of provision within the AG's resource DEL (Departmental Expenditure Limit) from TSol, CPS and RCPO. A similar reallocation will need to take place in 2006-07.

TSol also receives Voted funds to meet costs arising from its conduct of clients' legal work. These are known as operational costs and include payments to Counsel, expert witnesses and solicitor agents. The majority of these costs, estimated at £34m in 2006-07, are recovered from client Departments and the proceeds are Appropriated in Aid. Where such costs are incurred on cases undertaken in the general public interest, and are not therefore attributable to specific clients, they are charged to the Estimate (£2.7m in 2006-07).

Staff numbers show an increase as demand for TSol services grows. By introducing efficiencies, TSol has ensured that numbers have not increased at the same rate as demand. The levels of staff and the expenditure against each sub-head in the Estimate are summarised below:

Treasury Solicitor's Department	2002-03 Outturn	2003-04 Outturn	2004-05 Outturn	2005-06 Estimated	2006-07 Plans	2007-08 Plans
Core staff numbers	528	605	652	719	719	719
Gross administration costs	36,745	42,967	48,405	55,306	57,281	59,781
AGO						
Core staff numbers	33	36	41	50	50	50
Gross administration costs	3,066	3,312	3,908	4,212	3,720	3,720
HMCPSI						
Core staff numbers	44	43	46	52	52	52
Gross administration costs	3,278	3,485	3,382	3,971	3,971	3,971

Departmental Investment Strategy

The Department's investment strategy is directly linked to achieving its objectives. The total net book value of the Department's tangible fixed assets at 31 March 2005 was £28.3m, comprising £25.8m land and buildings and £0.8m IT equipment and furniture. This is expected to reduce to £6.5m by 31 March 2006 following the disposal of Queen Anne's Chambers, rising to £8.8m by 31 March 2006.

In 2005-06 TSol has continued its policy of investing in improving and developing systems to support its business. In particular, investment has been made in the following areas:

- The purchase of furniture and IT equipment required for the relocation to the new offices at One Kemble Street;
- Investment in the development and implementation of the electronic document and records management system (eRIK);
- Investment in the initial projects identified in the new IS Strategy.

Forward Look

2006-07 will be a financially challenging year. TSol's core clients are under greater financial pressure than ever, although the complexity of their cases increases. To improve business performance and deliver tangible benefit to clients, TSol must invest wisely to reduce the costs of the business, be creative about work organisation and deliver more from finite resources.

TSol must build upon its reputation for providing high quality legal services and work for even higher standards.

All elements of TSol service, from billing and invoicing to the delivery of legal expertise, will be scrutinised. TSol must improve business processes, information systems, infrastructure and leadership capability. There will be difficult decisions to make about use of resources and the focus must be on improvements that benefit TSol clients. TSol must continue to strengthen working relationships with clients, understanding their businesses better, in order to manage risk more effectively and reduce their legal costs. TSol will maintain tight control of future charge-out rates and the disbursement costs incurred by clients.

Further Information

Further information on the work of the Treasury Solicitor's Department may be obtained at www.tsol.gov.uk or from:

Business Strategy Unit
Treasury Solicitor's Department
One Kemble Street,
London WC2B 4TS

Telephone 020 7210 3571

www.tsol.gov.uk

ATTORNEY GENERAL'S OFFICE

Introduction

Role

The Attorney General's Office (AGO) is a separate department, for which the Treasury Solicitor is the Accounting Officer. AGO supports the Attorney-General and the Solicitor-General (Law Officers) as Ministers, in their wide-ranging, traditional functions of the government's chief legal advisers, in their Criminal Justice System (CJS) policy, finance and performance roles and in handling a large volume of legal casework.

Casework

Casework covers items such as:

- Referring unduly lenient sentences to the Court of Appeal;
- Consents to prosecutions;
- Bringing proceedings for contempt of court;
- Taking action against vexatious litigants;
- Intervening in the public interest in certain charity and family law cases;
- Appointing advocates to act for the Crown, as well as appointing 'advocates to the court', and 'special advocates' to represent the interests of appellants in cases involving sensitive material.

Policy, Finance and Performance

Working with the Law Officers' Departments, the Police and Administration Team identifies and leads or co-ordinates action on new policy initiatives e.g. fraud and international strategy and on those arising within the CJS e.g. the Fundamental Legal Aid Review and more recently Lord Carter's Review, new proposals for handling rape cases and the recently announced police restructuring proposals. It is also the point of liaison with CJS Agencies and OCJR, particularly in relation to the CJS initiatives for which the Attorney General and Solicitor General act as champions e.g. Operation Turn-Up ensuring defendants appear at court, European and on expert witness issues.

During the year, the Attorney General and the Chief Secretary to the Treasury jointly commissioned a wide-ranging review of fraud which is due to report in the late Spring. The Attorney General and the Law Officers' Departments have been working with other government departments on a more strategic approach to International issues. This work will be reflected in the international strategy for the Law Officers' Departments currently being developed.

In co-operation with the Law Officers' Departments Finance Directors' Groups, the team co-ordinates action on cross-Departmental finance and performance matters including those arising from the Comprehensive Spending Review 2007 and which have cross-CJS impact e.g. asset recovery. Significant, following the Spending Review 2004, has been concerted action in delivery of the Law Officers' Departments efficiency programmes.

Organisation

AGO is headed by the Legal Secretary, Jonathan Jones and has three separate areas of business: policy and administration, civil legal advice and criminal legal advice.

Management Structure

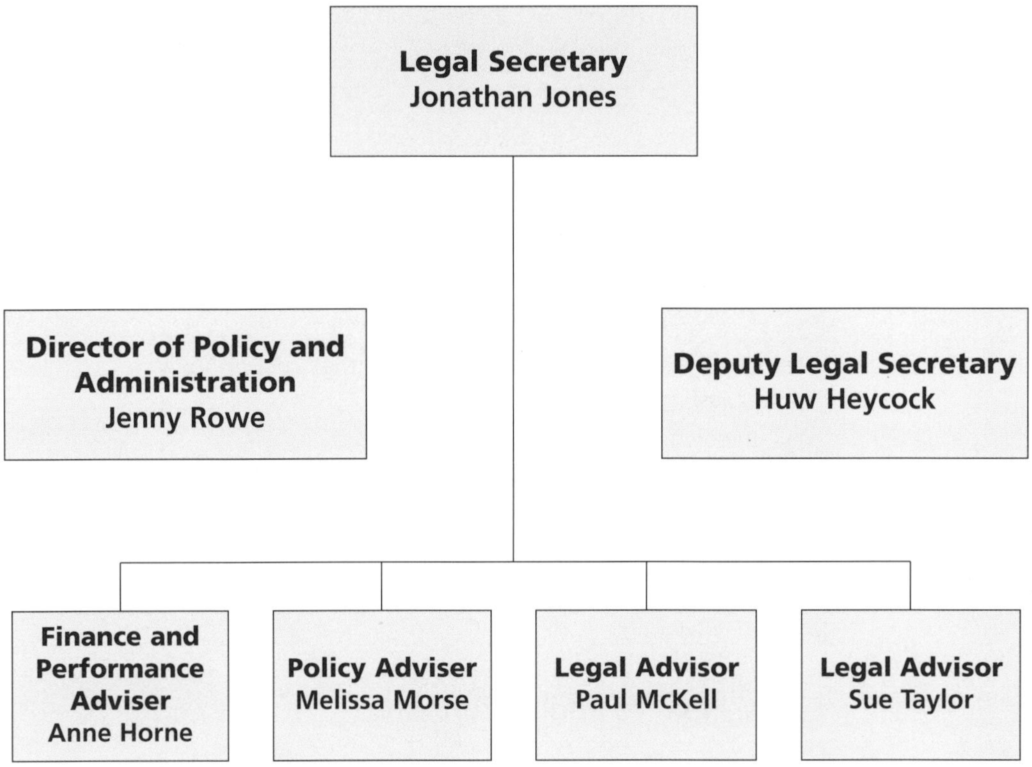

Aim

AGO contributes to the Attorney General's aim for all his departments of providing a world-class public service. In its support of the Law Officers, it contributes to all six service and developmental priorities of the Attorney General's strategy.

Objectives

AGO's strategic objectives are:

- To provide high quality and timely legal advice to the Law Officers to enable them to advise Ministers and other government departments;
- To provide high quality and timely policy advice, through a process of constructive engagement with other departments;
- To support the Law Officers' ministerial responsibilities in the criminal justice system, including the delivery of policy initiatives and trilateral performance targets;

- To deal with casework in a timely and appropriate way;
- To drive the joining up of the Law Officers' Departments so as to increase efficiency and effectiveness;
- To support the Law Officers in their oversight of the GLS; and in their general superintendence of prosecution work across government departments.

Targets

Historically the nature of the Office's work has been to respond to high demand in respect of both casework, policy advice and correspondence. Targets have not therefore been set but this aspect has been considered for introduction in 2006-07.

Performance

People

At the end of December 2005, AGO had some 50 staff, of which 18 were lawyers, 6 advised on policy or performance or handling correspondence, and 6 worked in the Ministers' Private Offices.

Workload

Overall the workload pressure on the Office continued to increase during 2005-06, particularly in relation to Ministers involvement in the work of the CJS.

Correspondence

In 2005 some 1,278 items of correspondence were answered of which 120 were Freedom of Information requests.

Finance

The AGO is funded as part of the Treasury Solicitor's Department Estimate. Its total provision is some £4m which, subject to final figures, is likely to be fully committed in 2005-06. The new finance capacity has continued to improve financial management information within the Office as well as providing advice on financial matters across the Law Officers' Departments and within the CJS.

Information Technology

During 2005-06 the Office improved its IT function by developing the capacity to move to the general Government Secure Intranet as well as the x-GSI connexion. It also together with the Serious Fraud Office renegotiated its IT supplier contract.

Sustainable Development

AGO is setting in place plans to improve its delivery of services to meet the government's sustainable development programme.

Forward Look

AGO expects to move accommodation in 2006-07 and alternative premises are under consideration.

Further Information

Further information can be obtained from:

The Attorney General's Office
9 Buckingham Gate
London SW1E 6JP

Telephone: 020 7271 2400

Website: www.lslo.gov.uk

HM CROWN PROSECUTION SERVICE INSPECTORATE

Introduction

HM Crown Prosecution Service Inspectorate (HMCPSI) was established as an independent statutory body by the Crown Prosecution Service Inspectorate Act 2000, which came into effect on 1st October 2000. The Chief Inspector is appointed by and reports to the Attorney General. He is an Additional Accounting Officer within the TSol Estimate with responsibility for HMCPSI expenditure.

HMCPSI maintains a risk register which is regularly reviewed. It was initially developed through a consultative process involving groups of staff at all levels in order to ensure that all potential risks were captured and assessed. Its revision has similarly been broadly based. The process of developing the HMCPSI Strategy and Business Plan for 2006-2008 included an extensive consultative exercise with internal and external stakeholders (including focus groups) and then was used to inform the business planning process and the necessary actions to manage the risks were incorporated into the HMCPSI Business Plan 2006-07. This position will be kept under review and modified as appropriate throughout the year. In particular the Inspectorate Management Team identified risks associated with the transition to the proposed single inspectorate which are constantly being monitored.

The processes described above have ensured a good level of awareness of risk within the Inspectorate. These inform the internal controls of HMCPSI. The most recent formal audit action was a follow-up review in April 2003 which concluded that a Level 1 Assurance was appropriate in April 2003. This reflected the view that the identified risks were then being effectively managed. The steps subsequently taken were intended to preserve that position.

Role

HMCPSI has a statutory obligation to report to the Attorney General on the performance of the Crown Prosecution Service. This obligation is fulfilled through the undertaking of a wide range of inspection activities. These include inspections of each of the CPS business units, as well as conducting thematic reviews of a range of specific issues on a national basis. The Inspectorate also collaborates with the other criminal justice inspectorates to examine specific issues on a thematic basis throughout the CJS. In addition it participates in a programme of inspection of criminal justice areas and undertaken jointly by the five criminal justice inspectorates.

With effect from April 2005, the statutory remit of HMCPSI was extended by the Commissioners for Revenue and Customs Act 2005, section 42 to include the Revenue and Customs Prosecution Office although a defect in legislation means that inspection cannot take place until the provisions of the Justice and Police Bill (currently before Parliament) have been enacted and implemented. The Justice (Northern Ireland) Act 2002 also provides for the Chief Inspector of Criminal Justice for Northern Ireland to delegate to HMCPSI functions relating to prosecution in Northern Ireland. Its findings are published through individual reports based on each inspection, and an Annual Report on the performance of the CPS is submitted to the Attorney General and laid before Parliament.

Management Structure

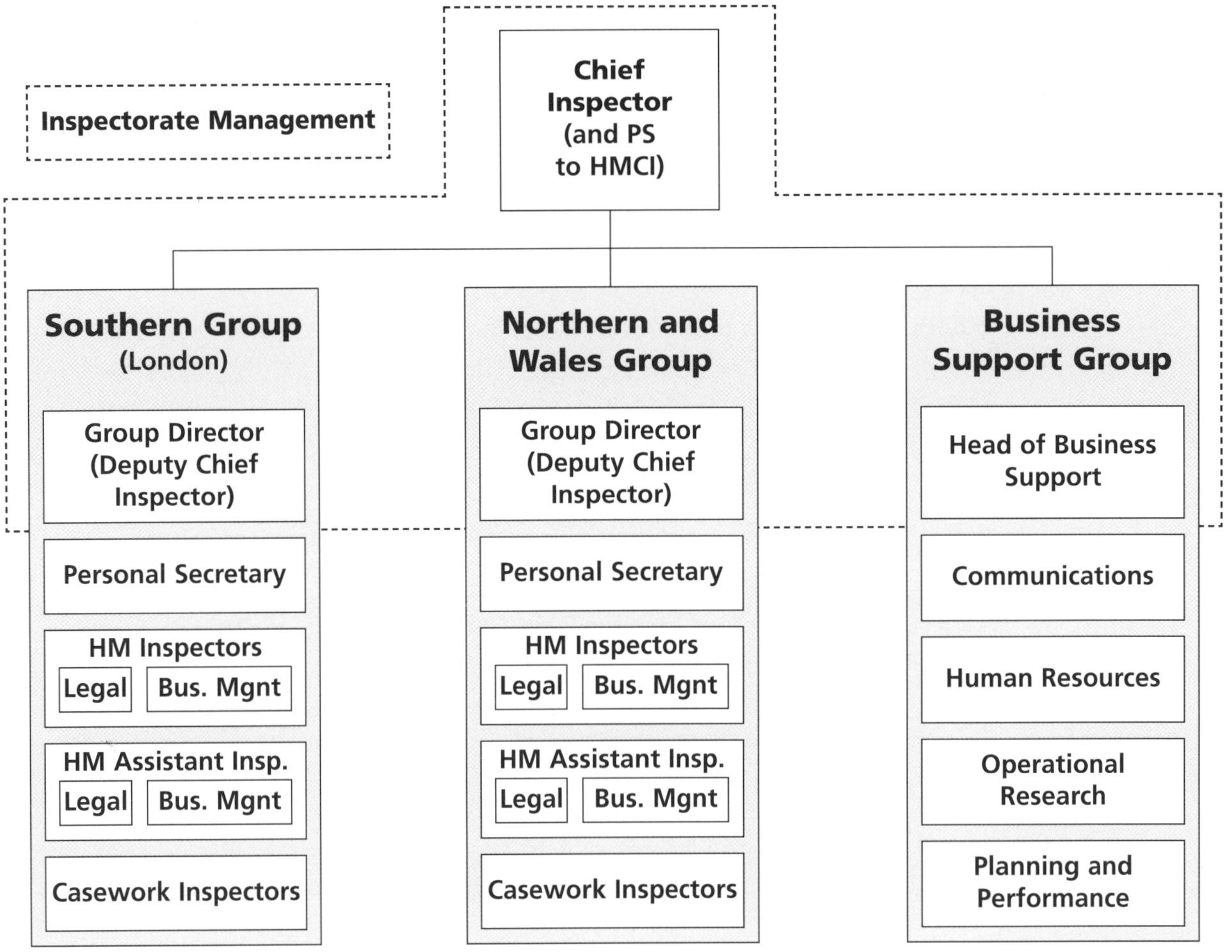

HMCPSI Performance

Mission and Objective

HMCPSI's mission statement, as set out in the 2005-06 Business Plan, is that:

> *HMCPSI strives to achieve excellence in all aspects of its activities and in particular to provide customers and stakeholders with consistent and professional inspection and evaluation processes together with advice and guidance, all measured against recognised quality standards and defined performance levels.*

The principal role of HMCPSI is to focus on outcomes that promote the effectiveness, efficiency and value for money of the CPS within a joined-up criminal justice system. HMCPSI meets this strategic objective by:

- Bringing about improvement through acting as a major driver for increasing performance in the prosecution functions that it is responsible for inspecting;.
- Encouraging joined-up working within the criminal justice system;
- Providing assurances to the Attorney General, DPP and CPS Chief Executive as to the performance of the CPS; and.
- Contributing to greater value for money within the CPS and the criminal justice system.

This approach applies equally but with appropriate adaptation to other bodies which it inspects.

Modernising HMCPSI

The Attorney General's Vision

HMCPSI supports the Attorney General's vision by strengthening HMCPSI's capability to deliver the key objectives as set out in our business plan and through a rigorous inspection programme, building strong relationships across government, particularly with other criminal justice inspectorates and our stakeholders, and by taking positive steps to strengthen its position as an employer of choice.

Strengthening Capability to Deliver

HMCPSI completed its second cycle of inspections in November 2004 with the last report being published in March 2005. It has also undertaken a series of progress follow-up visits to each of the 42 CPS Areas to assess the effectiveness of Area responses to recommendations in the second cycle reports and how aspects for improvement have been addressed.

Although it was not previously the practice to publish the reports of these visits, those completed from June 2005 have been published. Wherever possible follow-up visits in 2005-06 were combined with the overall performance assessment visits referred to below in order to make efficient use of resources and reduce the burden of inspection on CPS Areas.

During HMCPSI's second cycle of inspections (2002-04) the Attorney General asked that consideration be given to a scheme of overall performance assessments leading to a form of standard assessment which might be published. This approach reflected government thinking in relation to the accountability of public services that citizens are entitled to expect. The process was to produce a straightforward assessment of the quality of the public services being delivered in each CPS Area. This follows the practice of a number of inspectorates and commissions, relating to local government, police and health services. This has now been done. It has provided an opportunity to revise our inspection strategy by creating a baseline by which to compare and measure performance. Provided this baseline is kept up to date through gathering of management and other information relevant to performance, it will pave the way for a more risk-based approach to Area effectiveness inspections, focusing inspectorate resources where they are likely to make a real difference and freeing up staff to undertake more joint and cross-cutting thematic work.

HMCPSI chose a system of largely free-standing overall performance assessments, with the objective to secure a snap-shot of Area performance against clearly defined and strict standards across the 42 CPS Areas as close to simultaneously as its resources permitted.

HMCPSI have adopted the four commonly understood descriptors of:

Excellent – 4; Good – 3; Fair – 2; Poor – 1

CRITICAL ASPECTS OF PERFORMANCE	OTHER DEFINING ASPECTS
Pre-charge decision-making	Managing magistrates' courts cases
Ensuring successful outcomes	Managing Crown Court cases
Leadership	Handling sensitive cases and hate crimes
Service to victims and witnesses	Custody time limits
Managing resources	Disclosure
	Presenting/progressing cases at court
	Delivering change
	Managing performance to improve
	Securing community confidence

Within the overall performance assessment, 14 key performance aspects have been identified. These are divided into five critical aspects, which provide the basis of a combined assessment for these critical aspects, together with nine other defining aspects of performance.

Each aspect of performance was rated separately so that Areas can immediately identify their strengths and weaknesses. Thus, whilst Areas need to maintain their overall level of performance, they can, following the assessment, take action to address weaker points. This enables them to raise the standard of service to the public in key aspects. They can prioritise their effort and resources to deal with key issues whether they relate to casework, national initiatives or key targets with the Public Service Agreement shared between several criminal justice agencies.

The individual assessments of each of the 14 aspects also enables strengths and weaknesses across the CPS as a whole to be identified, so helping the CPS Business Development Directorate to target issues and best marshall effort and resources.

This new Overall Performance Assessment (OPA) process has, for the first time, provided a snap-shot overview of the performance of all 42 CPS Areas at one given time. As well as providing an assessment of the performance across the service the OPA process it has facilitated the identification of the Areas where further work is likely to give the biggest return on increased value for money; those that are furthest behind the best performers.

The evidence gathering process for the Overall Performance Assessments was substantially based on the CPS Area's self-assessment. This was tested by scrutiny of a wide range of management information and documentation, and a rigorous 'check and challenge' process with the management team during a short focused on-site visit.

The DPP and the Chief Executive have set out their expectations as to how the CPS will build on this process:

- *'Excellent' Areas will aim both to maintain their excellent rating and to increase the categories of performances rated as excellent.*
- *'Good' Areas will aspire to move to the excellent category. This means improving those categories rated as fair and establishing excellent performance in critical aspects of work.*
- *'Fair' Areas will aim to move to 'good'. This means focussing on those aspects rated as fair with immediate attention being given to any aspects rated as poor.*
- *'Poor' Areas must move to the 'fair' category. This means providing immediate attention to those critical aspects rated as poor within the next six months and attending to poor non-critical aspects within 12 months.*

This is a good illustration of how the CPS are using the work of HMCPSI to help drive improvement.

Resources

The costs of HMCPSI are met from the Estimate of the Treasury Solicitor's Department. The Inspectorate has budgeted for 52 members of staff during 2005-06.

The introduction of the Overall Performance Assessment process has been part of a wider change programme. This programme is intended to improve efficiency and effectiveness in inspection within HMCPSI, including the development of a methodology intended to maximize the benefit of the information gathered through the Overall Performance Assessment exercise, and this work is progressing well. The outcome of the Overall Performance Assessments will be used together with other measurement and performance information to inform a programme of Area Effectiveness Inspections. This programme will focus on the Areas which represent the higher risk and individual inspections are likely to be tailored to focus on the aspects of performance which are an issue.

The HMCPSI's strategy is to free up resources from cyclical Area work by this more risk informed approach so that a greater proportion of its resources are available for joint and cross-cutting work. HMCPSI plan further work in relation to the Revenue and Customs Prosecution Office and with the Criminal Justice Inspectorate for Northern Ireland.

HMCPSI Reports Published During 2005-06

OPA reports

First tranche published December 2005:

22 CPS Area reports, plus summary report of first tranche. The 22 Areas were: Bedfordshire, Cheshire, Cleveland, Cumbria, Devon & Cornwall, Derbyshire, Dorset, Durham, Dyfed Powys, Gloucestershire, Greater Manchester, Gwent, Humberside, Kent, Lancashire, Lincolnshire, Norfolk, Northumbria, North Wales, North Yorkshire, South Yorkshire and Warwickshire.

Second tranche published March 2006: The 20 Areas were: Avon & Somerset, Cambridgeshire, Essex, Hampshire & Isle of Wight, Hertfordshire, Leicestershire, Merseyside, Northamptonshire, Nottinghamshire, Staffordshire, South Wales, Suffolk, Surrey, Sussex, Thames Valley, West Mercia, West Midlands, West Yorkshire, Wiltshire, and London, consisting of London South Sector, London North and East Sector, London West Sector, Serious Casework and an overall London report.

The above were accompanied by the National Summative Report published March 2006.

Follow-up Inspections

Hampshire & Isle of Wight, Warwickshire, South Wales, Bedfordshire, Essex, Thames Valley, Lincolnshire, Devon & Cornwall, Greater Manchester, North Wales, Cumbria, Gwent, Staffordshire, Sussex, West Midlands, Hertfordshire, Avon & Somerset, Wiltshire and Surrey.

Thematic Reports

Bringing Back Quality of Life to our Communities: A Review of the Performance of the Crown Prosecution Service in Relation to Dealing with Social Impact Crime and Anti-Social Behaviour;
A Review of the Crown Prosecution Service Casework Quality Assurance Scheme;
Review of the use of Performance Information in the CPS;
A Review of the Role and Contribution of the Crown Prosecution Service to the Safeguarding of Children.

Joint[5] Inspection CJS Area Reports

Merseyside (August 2005); HMCPSI lead, with HMIC, HMI Prisons, HMI Probation, and HMICA. Gwent (February 2006); HMIC lead, with HMCPSI, HMICA, HMI Prisons, HMI Probation. Thames Valley (February 2006); HMICA lead, with HMCPSI, HMIC, HMI Prisons, and HMI Probation. Greater Manchester (completed and awaiting publication); HMIC lead, with HMCPSI, HMICA HMI Prisons, and HMI Probation. Northumbria (completed and awaiting publication) HMICA lead, with HMCPSI, HMIC, HMI Prisons, and HMI Probation.

Joint Thematic Reports

Joint Chief Inspectors' Report on Arrangements to Safeguard Children.
In progress:
Review of the Investigation and Prosecution of Rape Offences in England and Wales Follow-up.

[5] HMIC: HM Inspectorate of Constabulary, HMICA: HM Inspectorate of Courts Administration.

Chief Inspectors Annual Report 2004-05

Published 14 July 2005

Jubilee Line Fraud Case Review

This review, commissioned by the Attorney General under section 2(1)(b) of the Crown Prosecution Service Inspectorate Act 2000, has been reported to the Attorney General and will be published substantially contemporaneously with this report. It has been funded out of HMCPSI's existing resources.

Further Information

Further information may be obtained from:

HMCPSI
26-28 Old Queen Street
London SW1H 9HP

Telephone: 020 7210 1197

www.hmcpsi.gov.uk

Common Core Tables

Total public spending for the HM Procurator General and Treasury Solicitor								£'000
Consumption of resources	**2000-01 Outturn**	**2001-02 Outturn**	**2002-03 Outturn**	**2003-04 Outturn**	**2004-05 Outturn**	**2005-06 Estimate**	**2006-07 Plans**	**2007-08 Plans**
Providing comprehensive & competitive legal services to government departments & publicly funded bodies	9,272	10,127	9,625	8,940	15,722	14,205	13,169	13,169
Total Resource Budget [1]	**9,272**	**10,127**	**9,625**	**8,940**	**15,722**	**14,205**	**13,169**	**13,169**
Of which								
Resource DEL[1]	9,272	10,127	9,625	8,940	15,722	14,205	13,169	13,169
Capital Spending								
Providing comprehensive & competitive legal services to government departments & publicly funded bodies	585	1,189	1,807	2,149	2,227	4,750	4,000	4,000
Total Capital Budget	**585**	**1,189**	**1,807**	**2,149**	**2,227**	**4,750**	**4,000**	**4,000**
Of which								
Capital DEL[1]	585	1,189	1,807	2,149	2,227	4,750	4,000	4,000
Total public spending [2]	**8,938**	**10,303**	**10,557**	**9,802**	**14,410**	**17,455**	**15,569**	**15,069**

(1) Departmental Expenditure Limits, set as part of the 2004 Spending Review
(2) Total public spending calculated as the total of the resource budget plus the capital budget, less depreciation

Capital employed for the HM Procurator General and Treasury Solicitor								£'000
	2000-01 Outturn	**2001-02 Outturn**	**2002-03 Outturn**	**2003-04 Outturn**	**2004-05 Outturn**	**2005-06 Estimated**	**2006-07 Projected**	**2007-08 Projected**
Assets on balance sheet at end of year:								
Fixed Assets								
Intangible	–	348	1,041	173	590	575	975	1,175
Tangible	27,155	28,170	27,493	28,522	28,269	6,500	8,500	10,200
of which:								
Freehold Land and Buildings	26,070	29,968	26,119	24,874	25,808	–	–	–
Leasehold Land and Buildings	558	571	550	522	538	–	–	–
Development under Construction	–	–	–	2,423	1,046	70	1,000	1,000
Development in use	–	–	–	106	52	2,500	3,700	5,000
Computer Network	479	593	776	533	783	1,100	1,300	1,300
Fixtures and Fittings	48	38	48	64	41	2,200	2,500	2,900
Current Assets:	29,796	20,002	19,059	18,706	18,089	17,570	18,870	19,370
Creditors (<1 year)	–23,709	–13,516	–13,506	–9,427	–8,978	–11,005	–11,455	–11205
Creditors (>1 year)	–	–	–	–	–	–	–	–
Provisions	–4,504	–4,062	–3,811	–3,261	–3,123	–3,340	–2,840	–2,440
Capital Employed in Department	28,738	30,942	30,276	34,713	34,846	10,300	14,050	17,100
NDPB net assets	–	–	–	–	–	–	–	–
Capital employed in Department	28,738	30,942	30,276	34,713	34,846	10,300	14,050	17,100

Administration Budget HM Procurator General and Treasury Solicitor								£'000
	2000-01 Outturn	2001-02 Outturn	2002-03 Outturn	2003-04 Outturn	2004-05 Outturn	2005-06 Estimated	2006-07 Plans	2007-08 Plans
Administration Expenditure								
Paybill	19,712	24,458	28,269	39,128	41,113	45,008	47,226	48,987
Other	8,861	12,040	14,820	10,636	13,505	18,481	17,746	18,486
Total	**28,573**	**36,498**	**43,089**	**49,764**	**54,618**	**63,489**	**64,972**	**67,472**
Administrative Income	–23,515	–29,923	–35,026	–42,219	–42,246	–51,981	–54,500	–57,000
Total	**5,058**	**6,575**	**8,063**	**7,545**	**12,372**	**11,508**	**10,472**	**10,472**
Analysis by activity	5,058	6,575	8,063	7,545	12,372	11,508	10,472	10,472
Providing comprehensive & competitive legal services to government departments & publicly funded bodies								
Total Administration Budget	**5,058**	**6,575**	**8,063**	**7,545**	**12,372**	**11,508**	**10,472**	**10,472**

STAFF NUMBERS	Staff-years							£'000
Consumption of resources	2000-01 Actual	2001-02 Actual	2002-03 Actual	2003-04 Actual	2004-05 Actual	2005-06 Estimated	2006-07 Plans	2007-08 Plans
Treasury Solicitor's Department								
CS FTEs	461	490	586	664	717	801	801	801
Overtime	1	3	2	3	3	3	3	3
Casuals	29	30	19	20	22	20	20	20
Total	**491**	**523**	**607**	**687**	**742**	**824**	**824**	**824**

Printed in the UK by The Stationery Office Limited
on behalf of the Controller of Her Majesty's Stationery Office
ID 184555 05/06 334552 19585